on track ...

Crosby, Stills & Nash

every album, every song

Andrew Wild

SONICBOND

sonicbondpublishing.com

Sonicbond Publishing Limited
www.sonicbondpublishing.co.uk
Email: info@sonicbondpublishing.co.uk

First Published in the United Kingdom 2020
First Published in the United States 2020

British Library Cataloguing in Publication Data:
A Catalogue record for this book is available from the British Library

ISBN 978-1-78952-039-2

Typeset in ITC Garamond & ITC Avant Garde
Printed and bound in England

Graphic design and typesetting: Full Moon Media

Also by Andrew Wild:
108 Steps Around Macclesfield (Sigma Press, 1994 / 2nd edition, Rumble Strips, 2018)
Exploring Chester (Sigma Press, 1996 / re-publication, Rumble Strips, 2018)
Ever Forward (MADS, 1997)
Play On (Twelfth Night, 2009)
One for the Record (Avalon, 2013 / 2nd edition, 2018)
The Difficult Crossing (Stagescripts, 2016)
Pink Floyd Song by Song (Fonthill, 2017)
Queen On Track (Sonicbond, 2018)
The Beatles: An A-Z Guide to Every Song: On Track (Sonicbond, 2019)
Solo Beatles 1969-1980 On Track (Sonicbond, 2020)
James Bond On Screen (Sonicbond, 2021)
Dire Straits On Track (Sonicbond, 2021)
Fleetwood Mac in the 1970s (Sonicbond, 2021)

Acknowledgements

Thank you to Alan Pattinson, Debbie Kruger and Nick Clemson.
With love to Amanda, Rosie and Amy.

This one's dedicated to the memory of AR 'Bob' Murphy.
We lost another one.

One can't deny what has happened to us in the past.
The secret is to enjoy and be proud of the music we've created and the people with whom we have been linked. It's all a long chain of involvement in the world.
Graham Nash, interviewed by Debbie Kruger, 1999.

on track ...

Crosby, Stills & Nash

Contents

Introduction

For me, it started in Oban, Scotland, in 1983.

Aged 17, I had read about Crosby, Stills, Nash and Young in my battered and well-thumbed 1977 edition of *The Illustrated 'New Musical Express' Encyclopaedia of Rock*, which I'm fairly certain was given to me by my school librarian a year or two beforehand. I soaked up every word of that book. The first album I heard by any of them was *Everybody Knows This Is Nowhere*, courtesy of a knock-off Saudi cassette lent by my long-term pal Nick Clemson. Imagine, the first Neil Young song I ever heard was 'Cinnamon Girl'...

And then, on that Scottish holiday, I picked up a cassette copy of *So Far*, the first CSNY compilation album released in 1974. I'd like to think that it had been sitting there, in the rack of that Scottish record shop, for nine years. The album's eleven tracks comprised half of CSNY's entire studio output to date: 'Déjà Vu', 'Helplessly Hoping', 'Wooden Ships', 'Teach Your Children', 'Ohio', 'Find the Cost of Freedom', 'Woodstock', 'Our House', 'Helpless', 'Guinnevere', 'Suite: Judy Blue Eyes'. That's a strong line-up for any album. I was hooked and started to piece together their group and solo releases, mostly on vinyl, some as cassette copies. By age 19 I was collecting CSNY bootlegs: a triple-vinyl set of CSNY at Oakland in July 1974 comes to mind. I've been lucky enough to see CSN twice, and Neil Young twice, once with Crazy Horse. The Crosby-Nash, Stephen Stills and Graham Nash concerts I've seen in Manchester since 2005 have been sublime.

Crosby, Stills and Nash have released nearly fifty studio and live albums as solo artists, duos, trios and as a quartet with Neil Young. Add eight by The Hollies, six by The Byrds, three by Buffalo Springfield and two by The Rides then you have close to 800 songs. This is before we add over fifty solo albums by Neil Young, which are mercifully out of scope of this book.

Crosby, Stills and Nash On Track filters down this massive discography to their eight studio releases and three key live albums, examining each of these track by track. There is an opening chapter which explains how they came to work together and highlights the key songs from their work between 1963 and 1969. Compilations, archive releases and DVDs are also included in a separate chapter.

A further chapter discusses their many unfinished albums and solo and duo work outside the band's group releases, and there is a checklist of the 300 essential songs you'll need to listen to if you want to gain a full understanding of their remarkable collective careers.

Ignore the egos, the tantrums, the break-ups, the reconciliations, the drugs, the madness. Go back to the music, where it all began and, eventually, will be all that remains.

> 'It's really about the songs, man. The whole thing always comes down to the songs.'
> David Crosby interviewed by John Kwit and Dolf van Stijgeren, 2014

Andrew Wild, Rainow, Cheshire, 2020

CSN before CSN

1941: David Van Cortlandt Crosby was born in Los Angeles, on 14 August.
1942: Graham William Nash was born in Blackpool, on 2 February.
1945: Stephen Arthur Stills was born in Dallas, on 3 January.
1947: Nash meets Allan Clarke.
1956-1962: Nash and Clarke perform together as The Two Teens, the Guytones, Ricky and Dane and The Fourtones.
1962: David Crosby joins forces with singer Terry Callier in Chicago. They become part of the Greenwich Village scene in New York.
Nash and Clarke join Manchester band The Deltas.

Crosby joins Les Baxter's Balladeers, a conservative folk group. An album, *Les Baxter's Balladeers*, was released in 1963. Baxter himself, an easy-listening arranger and composer, was not part of the group.

Stills' earliest available recording: 'Travelin'', at Voice of America radio relay station in San Jose, Costa Rica.

The Deltas rename themselves The Hollies.

1963: Stephen Stills plays in a series of bands, including the Continentals which featured future Eagles guitarist Don Felder. He performs as a solo folk singer in New York.

Crosby leaves the Balladeers and joins the Los Angeles folk circuit. He records his first solo session.

The Hollies release their first three singles: '(Ain't That) Just Like Me', 'Searchin'' and 'Stay' (their first top 10 hit).

1964: Stephen Stills joins the Au Go-Go Singers.

Through Terry Callier, David Crosby meets Roger (then Jim), McGuinn. They form the Jet Set with Gene Clark and after watching the Beatles film *A Hard Day's Night*, add drummer Michael Clarke and bassist Chris Hillman to form The Beefeaters. The single 'Please Let Me Love You' / 'Don't Be Long' is released on 7 October but does not chart. They change their name to The Byrds.

The Hollies release three top ten singles: 'Just One Look', 'Here I Go Again' and 'We're Through' and the albums *Stay with The Hollies* and *In the Hollies Style*.

The Au Go-Go Singers album *They Call Us Au Go-Go Singers* is released. Stephen Stills sings lead vocals on one song: 'High Flying Bird'.

1965: The Byrds record 'Mr Tambourine Man' on 20 January. It is released on 12 April and reaches number one in both the United States and the United Kingdom.

Stills tours Canada as a member of The Company, a folk-rock group, and meets

Neil Young at the Fourth Dimension in Thunder Bay, Ontario.

The Hollies' single 'Yes I Will' is their fifth top ten hit in the UK, and they follow this up with their only number one, 'I'm Alive' and the album *Hollies*.

Crosby sings lead on the bridge in the Byrd's second single 'All I Really Want to Do', released in June alongside their debut album *Mr Tambourine Man*.

Stephen Stills moves to California, working as a session musician. He auditions, unsuccessfully, for The Monkees.

Graham Nash meets David Crosby during the Byrds' August tour of the United Kingdom.

'Look Through Any Window' provides The Hollies with another top tenner.

The Byrds' second US #1, 'Turn! Turn! Turn!' / 'She Don't Care About Time' is released on 1 October. The album *Turn! Turn! Turn!* is released in December.

The Byrds record their first versions of 'Eight Miles High' and its b-side 'Why', both co-written by David Crosby. Re-recordings are released on 14 March 1966.

1966: Stephen Stills and Neil Young form Buffalo Springfield after meeting when stuck in traffic on Sunset Boulevard on 6 April. Their live debut is five days later, and they tour as support for The Byrds soon after.

Gene Clark leaves The Byrds. Crosby's songwriting becomes more prolific, including 'What's Happening?!?!', released on The Byrds' third album, *Fifth Dimension*, released on 18 July.

Buffalo Springfield's debut single, Young's 'Nowadays Clancy Can't Even Sing' is released in August.

The Hollies release three top 5 singles in the UK ('I Can't let Go', 'Bus Stop' and 'Stop Stop Stop') and the albums *Would You Believe* and *For Certain Because*. The latter has Nash lead vocals on two songs.

Stills writes 'For What It's Worth' in November. Buffalo Springfield's self-titled debut follows in December.

1967: Crosby's trademark style starts to emerge on songs such as 'Renaissance Fair', 'Mind Gardens', 'Everybody's Been Burned' and 'It Happens Each Day', all recorded during sessions for *Younger Than Yesterday*, released on 6 February.

The Hollies achieve a further two top-five singles: 'On a Carousel' and 'Carrie Anne'. Their album *Evolution* comes out in June.

'For What It's Worth' hits the top ten in the US in March.

In June, Crosby performs with Buffalo Springfield at the Monterey Pop Festival, as well as appearing with The Byrds.

Crosby's 'Lady Friend' is released as a single by The Byrds on 13 July. It's their lowest-charting single to date.

Nash's 'King Midas in Reverse' is released as a single by The Hollies. It only reaches number eighteen, their first self-written single to miss the top ten. Their seventh album, *Butterfly*, is dominated by Nash who sings lead on several songs.

Stephen Stills meets Judy Collins at a Cream show at the Whisky a Go Go in San Francisco.

McGuinn and Hillman dismiss Crosby from the Byrds in October after he refused to record a cover of Goffin and King's 'Goin' Back' and insisted that the band record his menage-a-trois song 'Triad'.

Buffalo Springfield Again is released in November.

1968: The Hollies travel to California. Crosby and Nash resume their acquaintance and Nash meets Stephen Stills after a Valentine's Day show by The Hollies at the Whiskey a Go Go.

David Crosby and Stephen Stills start informally working together.

The Hollies release the single 'Jennifer Eccles' in March 1968, their last with Graham Nash. Nash meets Joni Mitchell.

The Hollies record Nash's 'Marrakesh Express' in London on 2 April 1968.

Buffalo Springfield perform their last gig, at Long Beach on 5 May. Stills records *Super Session* with Al Kooper soon after.

Crosby records acoustic demos of several songs with Doors producer Paul Rothchild including 'Games', 'Laughing', 'The Wall Song' and an early version of 'Wooden Ships'.

Crosby records a demo of 'Guinnevere' on 26 June. Crosby and Stills record a demo version of 'Long Time Gone' at around the same time. Stills tapes a demo of '49 Reasons'. These three recordings comprise the 'Frozen Noses' tape.

At a party in July 1968 at either Joni Mitchell's house (according to Crosby and Nash) or Cass Elliot's (Stills' recollection), Crosby, Stills and Nash sing together on Stills' 'You Don't Have to Cry'. Nash: 'That was the first song we ever sang together. It was in Joni Mitchell's living room.' Stills: 'No, it was at Cass Elliot's dining room table. In the corner in a stucco room, near the kitchen and the pool.' Crosby: 'Nope, sorry.' Stills: 'I would've never sung for the first time with you guys in front of Joni Mitchell. Well, she was too intimidating.' Crosby: 'You did.' Stills: 'I did not.' Crosby: 'You did.' Stills: 'The second time …' Crosby: 'The very first time.' Stills: 'I'm never giving this up ever 'cause I can smell it, I can remember.' Crosby: 'I don't care.' Nash: 'You don't have to.' Crosby: 'You can welcome to it, man, you're wrong. But it's okay, we love you anyway.' Stills: 'Yeah, well then quit with a smug look, 'cause you're wrong.' Crosby: 'No, I'm not.' Stills: 'We've been fighting about this for 40 years.'

The third and final Buffalo Springfield album *Last Time Around* comes out in July.

Stills records twelve songs after a Judy Collins session, including early versions of 'Suite: Judy Blue Eyes', 'Helplessly Hoping' and 'Wooden Ships'. These were released in 2007 and most likely date from Summer 1968. Judy Collins says it's July 1968.

Crosby and Stills fly to London to persuade Nash to move to the US.

Nash performs his last gig with the Hollies on 8 December 1968 and immediately flies to Los Angeles. The first CSN recording sessions take place later that month.

> I guess I'm taking a chance, moving out here to LA, leaving my money in England and singing with David and Stephen. But it's what I want. At least it is for now.
> Graham Nash, *Hit Parader*, September 1969

1969: Crosby, Stills & Nash

Personnel:
David Crosby: vocals, guitar
Stephen Stills: vocals, guitar, bass, keyboards, percussion
Graham Nash: vocals, guitar
and
Cass Elliot: backing vocals on 'Pre-Road Downs'
Jim Gordon: drums on 'Marrakesh Express'
Dallas Taylor: drums on 'Suite: Judy Blue Eyes', 'You Don't Have to Cry', 'Pre-Road Downs', 'Wooden Ships', 'Long Time Gone', '49 Bye-Byes'
Recorded February – March 1969, Wally Heider's Studio III. Produced by Crosby, Stills and Nash.
Released: 29 May 1969 (US). Highest chart positions: 6 (US), 25 (UK).

> It was amazing what their voices did together. The tightness was incredible. I don't think any of us were quite prepared for the power that came out of that blend. They would lean together around one mike and get takes with such ease.
> *Crosby, Stills & Nash* engineer Bill Halverson.

Whereas vocally, *Crosby, Stills & Nash* is a product of their three voices blending together, musically, it belongs almost entirely to Stephen Stills. If we remove the wholly acoustic 'Lady of the Island' and mostly acoustic 'Guinnevere', on which the songs' writers accompany themselves on guitar, Stephen Stills plays virtually all of the instruments on this album, apart from the drums and some electric rhythm guitar from Crosby. Stills proves his worth on lead guitar, bass, percussion and keyboards – they dubbed him 'Captain Manyhands' – with subtle colouring such as the backwards guitar of 'Pre-Road Downs' and the stereo organs of 'Marrakesh Express'.

Engineer Henry Lewy: 'Right away they started doing everything themselves. They were like little geniuses. At one point, Stills was playing drums, then guitar, then organ. I'd seen other multi-talented people before, but none as equally adept at every instrument.' Nash: 'I thought it was going to be an acoustic album. It had started out that way. But Stephen had other ideas.'

Crosby Stills & Nash was recorded mostly in February and March 1969 after earlier sessions in December 1968 failed to get the results they wanted. The songwriting is split evenly between the three of them and sets the tone for their subsequent solo careers: Crosby's odd tunings and self-opinionated imagery on 'Guinnevere' and 'Long Time Gone'; Stills' complex and expressive songs 'Suite: Judy Blue Eyes', 'Helplessly Hoping', 'You Don't Have to Cry' and '49 Bye-Byes'; Nash's heartfelt ballads and pop tunes 'Lady of the Island', 'Marrakesh Express', and 'Pre-Road Downs'. 'Wooden Ships' was a joint composition.

'We were in love with each other at the time we recorded that album,' Graham Nash says. 'We were new friends discovering new parts about each other and we had songs. And we had the ability to translate those songs into records that was astounding, and we knew it. When we walked out of the studio with that two-track under our arm, we knew what it was going to do. We knew that it was going to be a hit. We knew that we had nailed something that wasn't really that popular kind of then. It was all Led Zeppelin and Jimi Hendrix and stuff and here comes this little acoustic record.'

The album was recorded with drummer Dallas Taylor, who had been introduced to Stephen Stills through a mutual friend, the Lovin' Spoonful's John B Sebastian. 'I had heard that Stephen was looking for a drummer,' Taylor told *4waysite.com* in 2007. 'We did a demo of 'Suite: Judy Blue Eyes' with Doug Lubaun on bass. John [Sebastian] and I were working on his album when I met Graham Nash. Stills, Nash and Crosby were singing some background for John. They went to London to rehearse their vocals for an upcoming 'folk record' they were due to make for Atlantic, à la Peter Paul and Mary. We serendipitously met at Kennedy Airport. I arrived from LA. They arrived from London. We rode the same limo out to John's house where we were all going to stay. We jammed in John's studio and that's where they asked me to join. It went from folk to rock and roll with my joining the band.'

The influence of *Crosby Stills & Nash* was huge. Like *In the Court of the Crimson King* released a few months later and *Black Sabbath* early the following year, *Crosby Stills & Nash* was the first blossoming of a new type of music, one of the dominant popular music categories in America during the 1970s: in this case, the singer-songwriter. For the next several years, the US charts were full of often self-reflective, usually acoustic-based, sometimes country-tinged songs and albums, painstakingly arranged and recorded often with vocal harmonies. The acts were probably from (or resident in) California. Step forward The Eagles, James Taylor, Joni Mitchell, Jackson Browne, Bread, Neil Young, Linda Ronstadt, Cat Stevens, Poco, America, Firefall, Souther-Hillman-Furay Band, Loggins & Messina, Seals & Croft, Dan Fogelberg, post-1975 Fleetwood Mac ... and eventually to the likes of Warren Zevon, Suzanne Vega, Tracy Chapman, Fleet Foxes, David Gray, Ray LaMontagne, Jewel, Jack Savoretti and hundreds of others.

But first, a work of genius.

'Suite: Judy Blue Eyes' (Stills)

Released as a single (edited), September 1969. B-side 'Long Time Gone'. Highest chart positions: 21 (US).

Nash: 'Probably one of my favourite Crosby, Stills & Nash songs.' 'Suite: Judy Blue Eyes' is a truly magnificent song about Judy Collins that stands as Stills' *magnum opus*. It was written around the time Stills and Collins relationship came to an end – late Summer 1968 – and is rigorously self-examining: 'Don't let the past remind us of what we are not now'.

Stephen Stills: 'It was the beginnings of three different songs that suddenly fell together as one.'

The song was composed using the 'Bruce Palmer Modal Tuning' (look it up, guitar players) and has four distinct sections. The opening section, through to 2:56 is a more or less straightforward pop-folk song with four verses and the 'I am yours, you are mine, you are what you are' chorus. Stills takes the lead vocal with Crosby and Nash providing harmonies. The second section 2:56 to 4:43, performed in half time has four verses of three-part harmony ('Friday evening, Sunday in the afternoon / What have you got to lose?') and Stills' striking push into falsetto on 'It's my *heart* that's suffering'. The third section, 4:43 to 6:25 has poetic lyrics ('chestnut brown canary, ruby-throated sparrow') and those roof-lifting harmonies from Crosby and Nash. The final section is sung in Spanish, with 'doo-doo-doo-dun-do' backing vocals. For the record: '¡Que linda! Me la traiga a Cuba. La reina de la Mar Caribe. Quiero sólo visitarla allí. Y que triste que no puedo. ¡Vaya! O Va! O Va!' ... 'How lovely! Take me to Cuba. The queen of the Caribbean Sea. I want to just visit there. And how sad that I can't.'

> It started out as a long narrative poem about my relationship with Judy Collins. It poured out of me over many months and filled several notebooks. I had a hell of a time getting the music to fit. I was left with all these pieces of song and I said, 'Let's sing them together and call it a suite,' because they were all about the same thing and they led up to the same point. And the little kicker at the end about Cuba was just to liven it up because it had gone on forever and I didn't want it to just fall apart. I said, 'Now that we've sung all these lyrics about one thing, let's change the subject entirely.' And we did. Even did it in a different language just to make sure that nobody could understand it.
> Stephen Stills

Initial sessions leaked to collectors show that the basic take was Stills and drummer Dallas Taylor performing the entire track end-to-end ('could I have a little more Dallas please?', Stills asks). An alternative mix with a more audible drum track was released in 1991 on the *CSN* box set. A busier unreleased mix, with electric guitar lead lines throughout the opening section, circulates amongst collectors. There is also a that Summer 1968 solo demo (released on *Just Roll Tape* in 2007) where, without those soaring harmonies, Stills' vocal performance is fragile, exposed and heart-felt.

But the version of 'Suite: Judy Blue Eyes' that we know and love today was very nearly ditched at the last minute. During mixing, Stills decided that they needed a brand-new version. This was recorded start to finish in six hours. 'Then,' Nash commented later, 'we listened to the two versions and ended up using the original one. It was just better.'

A 4:36 single edit removes the second and fourth verses from the first section, the third and fourth verses from the second section, and the final verse from the third section.

'Suite Judy Blues Eyes' was performed as the band's opening number at the

Woodstock festival. Whilst not a constant in CSN(Y) setlists over the years, 'Suite Judy Blues Eyes' has always been a crowd-pleaser, combining Stills' phenomenal acoustic guitar technique with those thrilling vocal harmonies.

Judy Collins:

> I first heard it in a hotel room, somewhere. Either that or in my apartment. Stephen came in and sat down and started to play this song. And I started to cry. It's one of those pieces of music that is so of a time, and yet it's timeless. It's so rare to find something like that.

In 2011 'Suite: Judy Blue Eyes' was listed as the 418th greatest song of all time by *Rolling Stone*.

'Marrakesh Express' (Nash)

Released as a single, 1969. B-side 'Helplessly Hoping'. Highest chart positions: 28 (US), 17 (UK).

It's often been written that Graham Nash brought pop sensibilities to Crosby, Stills and Nash. Both Stills and Crosby had written or co-written top ten hits of their own, however: 'Eight Miles High' in 1966 and 'For What It's Worth' in 1967. But Nash was a more pure pop writer and the importance of the cross-over chart singles success of 'Marrakesh Express' and the forthcoming 'Our House', 'Teach Your Children', 'Just a Song Before I Go' and 'Wasted on the Way' should not be underestimated.

'Marrakesh Express' was inspired by a trip to Morocco in 1966. 'I was ... getting on a train and having a first-class ticket and then reali[sed] that the first-class compartment was completely fucking boring, you know, ladies with blue hair in there – it wasn't my scene at all. So I decide I'm going to go and see what the rest of the train is like. And the rest of the train was fascinating. Just like the song says, there were ducks and pigs and chickens all over the place and people lighting fires. It's literally the song as it is – what happened to me.'

Nash presented the song to The Hollies, but they weren't interested, which is a surprise as it's not so far removed from Hollies songs such as 'Carrie Anne', 'Sorry Suzanne', 'Stop Right There', 'Tell Me To My Face', 'Relax', 'Not That Way At All', 'Stop Stop Stop' and, especially, 'King Midas In Reverse'. The Hollies recorded a backing track at Abbey Road on 2 April 1968 and despite an advanced arrangement, it's clear that their hearts aren't in it.

The CSN version was recorded on 11 February 1969; Nash plays acoustic guitar, Jim Gordon is the drummer, Stills adds Hammond B3 organ, piano, bass and the distinctive two-part guitar riff.

'A train song,' Stills said in 1969, 'and it sounds like drunken Mexican cornet players in one part, but that's my guitar overdubbed twice.'

'Marrakesh Express' was released as a single in July 1969 (b-side, 'Helplessly

Hoping') reaching no. 28 on the Billboard Hot 100 on 23 August 1969, the week after the band's performance at Woodstock when they played it as 'a medley of our hit'. It has remained a setlist constant since then and is one of CSN(Y)'s most-performed and best-loved songs. The impact of 'Marrakesh Express' on the success of its parent album was significant.

A sprightly demo version, recorded at in London in November 1968 when Crosby, Stills and Nash first seriously worked together, just before Nash quit The Hollies, was released in 2018 on *Over the Years*.

'Guinnevere' (Crosby)

It's obvious that, by 1967, David Crosby's ambitions were too big for The Byrds. 'Everybody's Been Burned' from *Younger Than Yesterday* (February 1967) mapped Crosby's future path.

> One of the most haunting songs in The Byrds' catalogue, and one of David Crosby's finest compositions 'Everybody's Been Burned' contains a melody, lyric and arrangement in perfect synthesis. Lyrically, it's typical Crosby – unspecific, vague yet beautiful – 'Everybody knows and me / I know that door that shuts just before / You get to the dream you see'. The music is similarly gentle, with a gorgeous, Eastern sounding guitar part from [Roger] McGuinn and some great bass playing from Chris Hillman. However, it's David Crosby that's the star of the show – his vocal is tender, searching and immaculate. Arguably the highlight of Younger Than Yesterday.
> Thomas Ward, *Allmusic.com*

'Guinnevere' is not so far removed in tempo, tone or technique. Graham Nash:

> Crosby sent me a tape of 'Guinnevere' in 1968 and it was one of the things that [made me] really realize that this man was a profound thinker and a great musician. 'Guinnevere' and 'Déjà Vu' were on the same tape and it was then that I realized that Crosby was something special.

Crosby's stunning solo demo was recorded on 26 June 1968 and was first released on the 1991 *CSN* box set. A remixed version can be heard on the *Voyage* box set. Crosby:

> I love this version of 'Guinnevere' because of the beauty that Jack Casady [bass] and Cyrus Faryar [bouzouki] brought to it. That was delicious. I thought I was making a record at the time, but I didn't know for whom. I just got in the studio. I would have put the track on the first CSN album just as it is, but Stephen and Graham wanted me to try the song over again so they could add their own things to it. But Jack was such a brilliant and adventuresome player – he had incredible tone and sound, and played like no one else. A towering monster of a musician.

The final studio mix released on *Crosby, Stills & Nash* is just Crosby (vocals, acoustic and electric guitars) and Nash (vocals). The vocal parts are double-tracked. An alternative mix, with bass guitar, more backing vocals, a busy drum track, and a clean ending circulates amongst collectors. This version sounds a lot like The Byrds. The drum track can be heard, very low in the mix of the right stereo channel of the released mix during the opening seconds.

An unused wholly acoustic take has a 20-second guitar introduction chopped from the final arrangement and single-tracked vocals from Crosby and Nash. Crosby sings the 'Peacocks wandered aimlessly / underneath an orange tree' line with no vocal backing. Nash declares, at the end of the take 'I'd like to double the voices on that right now! Let's go, we're gonna kill it.' 'OK,' whispers Crosby. The chemistry between these two men is palpable: live performances of 'Guinnevere' were frequently sublime.

The song was later covered by Miles Davis, as Crosby recollected: 'He walked up to me outside the Village Gate. 'You Crosby?' I said, 'Yes, sir.' He said, 'I'm Miles.' I said, 'Oh, I know.' Then he said, 'I cut one of your tunes.' My heart stopped. I couldn't believe it. Did he just say . . . did he just . . . oh! [starts panting, fanning himself] He's cut 'Guinnevere'.'

In 2008, Crosby commented 'That is a very unusual song, it's in a very strange tuning [EBDGAD] with strange time signatures. It's about three women that I loved. One of whom was Christine Hinton, the girl who got killed who was my girlfriend, and one of whom was Joni Mitchell and the other one is somebody that I can't tell. It might be my best song.'

He might be right.

'You Don't Have to Cry' (Stills)

A beautiful acoustic country song, that sounds simple but shows musicianship of the highest order. It is sung in gorgeous three-part harmony except in the chorus when Crosby scats around the lyric and melody. Stills' understated guitar harmonics add musical depth to this song of hurt pride and love lost. The second verse is simply a repeat of the first.

> It was a letter that never got sent. I took bits and pieces of it, put them into a song and it got posted through the record business instead of the mail.

Nash: 'The first time we recorded it was in New York City at the Record Plant in December 1968.'

That version, more explicitly country in arrangement, was released in 1991 on the *CSN* box set. An earlier demo, just Stills and an acoustic guitar is on the *Demos* album (2009).

'Pre-Road Downs' (Nash)

A rock song from Nash, very 1969 in message and arrangement:

I have kissed you, so I'll miss you / On the road I'll be wantin' you / But I have you, 'cause I love you / And you have me 'cause you love me too, yeah.

In a wider sense, it's a song about the life changes that Nash has been experiencing. Session tapes of the basic take reveal Stephen Stills on organ and guide vocals, Nash strumming his electric guitar and Taylor on drums, with everything else added later. The backwards guitar is played by Stills. 'This is real backwards guitar, and how he got it to match up to the forwards stuff, I have no idea,' Nash said. 'He did it, and we looked him and thought, 'This guy is from fucking Mars!' I'm still freaked out by it.'

A lovely acoustic demo version recorded at Wally Heider's in February 1969 was released in 2018 on *Over the Years.* Nash has yet to write the lyrics 'Don't run the time approaches / Hotels and midnight coaches / Be sure to hide the roaches', but this version is full of life. Cass Elliot adds her own vocal contribution to these lines on the *Crosby, Stills & Nash* version.

'Wooden Ships' (Crosby / Kantner / Stills)

The hippiest song of all time? A post-apocalyptic science fiction story tracks the survivors of a nuclear holocaust in which the two sides have annihilated each other.

It started with two demo versions. Crosby's, from March 1968, has the chords for the verses and chorus with Crosby scat singing the melody but no lyrics as yet. David Crosby:

I'd been kicked out of the Byrds, and I found a boat and bought it, in Fort Lauderdale. Stephen came down to see me and Paul Kantner came down to see me, and they happened to be there at the same time. I had this set of changes that I'd been playing for a long time, that I really, really loved. We were sitting around in the main cabin of the boat, and we started fooling around, as we would naturally do, and we started playing that set of changes and we wrote that song together. Stephen came up with a couple of ways to arrange it, musically, and he wrote the 'Horror grips us as we watch you die' verse. Paul came up with the original hook line, 'Wooden ships on the water'. It was a very organic process; we really wrote it very, very together. I borrowed the first part off a little Baptist church sign in Florida that said 'If you smile at me I will understand because that is something everybody everywhere does in the same language.' I'm amazed we never wrote anything else together. It was such a kick in the head to do it. Paul continued writing and added an entire section to his version of it that we didn't. One of the things that I most liked was that we did it and they did it and then people would go out and buy both records and then play them back to back, and say, 'Well, dig, this is a, oh, now, here, well, I really like, but see here, and I really like when they do that.' It was a great thing. It's one of my most favourite Crosby, Stills and Nash songs. I really love what it says, I really love how unusual it is and I really love the harmonies. It's definitely a science fiction song, no question.

Stills' more advanced demo, with most of the words in place, can be heard on *Just Roll Tape*.

At Wally Heider's in Spring 1969, the basic track was recorded by Stills (acoustic guitar) and Taylor (drums). Stills added bass guitar, stinging lead guitar and organ; Crosby put down his idiosyncratic electric rhythm guitar and they all recorded some of their best vocals.

Jefferson Airplane recorded their own version with some different lyrics for the album *Volunteers*, released in November 1969. Jorma Kaukonen's lead guitar parts are quite astounding. Both Jefferson Airplane and CSNY performed the song in their respective sets at Woodstock. Note that the CSNY version that opens the film is a different studio take, with different drum fills amended timing/inflection on the vocals a discordant ending. This has never been officially released. 'My whole 'Wooden Ships,' wanting-to-sail-forever fantasy was bullshit,' Crosby would admit less than a decade later. 'Where do you get off leaving the rest of humanity behind, even in your mind? ... You live, you learn'.

Jackson Browne wrote and recorded a follow-up, 'For Everyman' on which Crosby sang. In 1986, Neil Young released the song 'Hippie Dream'. He sings: 'The tie-dye sails are the screaming sheets / And the dusty trail leads to blood in the streets / And the wooden ships are a hippie dream / Capsized in excess'. The lines 'Another flower child goes to seed in an ether-filled room full of meat-hooks / It's so ugly. So ugly.'

These lyrics are surely about David Crosby.

'Lady of the Island' (Nash)

Nash stakes his claim as a singing, songwriting, heart-on-his-sleeve troubadour on this direct, fragile, very gentle and slightly saccharine acoustic song. From here, the triumphs of his first solo album are just over the horizon. Some sources suggest that 'Lady of the Island' was written possibly as early as 1967, under the title 'Isle of Dew', and that the Hollies didn't want to record it. Graham Nash:

> It's a song for two ladies. The islands in question are Ibiza and Long Island. Warm gentle feelings. Recorded in one take, Crosby and I improvising that nice little fugue in the middle.

Session tapes reveal that there was a false start, but they didn't get past the opening line before stopping to try again. Nash also added a second lead vocal and Crosby a second pass at the counterpoint vocal, both of which were ultimately mixed out.

'Helplessly Hoping' (Stills)

Released as the b-side of 'Marrakesh Express', 1969.

Perfection in song. A simple-fingerpicked acoustic guitar, Am7-C-G-D, underpins supreme, poetic lyrics and peerless vocals. Nash:

> We wrote that with a lot of alliteration. The first time we recorded it was here in New York City at the Record Plant in December 1968. Paul Rothchild was helping us with the record. We did two songs: 'You Don't Have to Cry' and 'Helplessly Hoping.'

Crosby:

> I loved it as a song, and I loved what happened with it. We got very lucky, very fortunate with the harmonies on that one. They came out extremely well. We still play it every night.

Stills:

> This song was inspired a long time ago by my tenth-grade English teacher in Tampa, Florida. She was a real knock-out, so much so that she got all the football players to stand up and read poetry, trying to impress her with how sensitive we were and how much we loved this awful stuff. Some of it must've rubbed off on me.

Two other remarkable and quite different versions are available. Stills' demo, from Summer 1968, is just one voice and one guitar. The power of the song-writing is evident but it's clear just how much the harmonies would later add. A CSNY rehearsal from Sunwest Studios, LA, 15 June 1969, released in 1991, has the full 6-piece band, playing gently and reverentially on electric guitars, bass and drums.

The song's subject – Judy Collins, of course – has sung the song herself live.

'Long Time Gone' (Crosby)

Released as the b-side of 'Suite: Judy Blue Eyes', September 1969.

The tightly-wound 'Long Time Gone' was written on 6 June 1968. David Crosby:

> I wrote that right after they assassinated Bobby Kennedy. It was a result of losing him, of losing John Kennedy and Martin Luther King. I started to feel overwhelmed. It seemed as if it was ballot by bullet. It seemed as if it didn't matter how good a person we could find to put up as an inspiration and a leader for the good, that somehow the other side would triumph by simply gunning them down.

Graham Nash:

> The art of being a songwriter is to take an incident that happens to you personally and be able to translate that into something that everybody that listens to the songs can understand.

Crosby's irate demo, recorded with Stephen Stills' assistance probably only three or so weeks after the song was written, was heard on bootlegs for years before its official release on the *Voyage* box set in 2006. The chorus stutters rather than flows. Famously, during the sessions for the band's debut album, Stills re-arranged and simplified the chorus and stayed up all night with drummer Dallas Taylor to record a complete instrumental backing track – organ, bass and guitar. They unveiled it to Crosby and Nash the following day.

'When we came back and heard the playback,' Crosby wrote in his memoirs, 'I just sat there, stunned.' Suitably incentivised, Crosby immediately laid down that tremendous, unhinged lead vocal part in five enervating takes. A classic of the era is born.

A very different mix was used on the soundtrack to the *Woodstock* film – this alternative version has never been commercially released.

'49 Bye-Byes' (Stills)

The cuckoo in the nest– the only song on the album which hasn't yet been established as a classic song on its own right. It perhaps sounds too much like late-period Buffalo Springfield– it has clear echoes of 'Four Days Gone' from *Last Time Around*, a link which is much more explicit if you listen to '49 Bye-Byes' on *4 Way Street* and 'Four Days Gone' on *Stephen Stills Live*.

'49 Bye-Byes' is a break-up song, tightly performed, beautifully sung but ultimately shallow. It's a combination of two song fragments, '49 Reasons' and 'Bye Bye Baby', hence '49 Bye-Byes'. Stills' 1968 'Frozen Noses' demo of '49 Reasons' can be heard on the *Carry On* box set. On all releases prior to 2006, David Crosby sings an excerpt of 'Come on in My Kitchen' between 'Long Time Gone' and '49 Bye-Byes'. This was removed at the request of the late Robert Johnson's estate.

2006 re-issue bonus tracks

'Do for the Others' (Stills)

Three of the bonus tracks on the 2006 re-issue date from 17 November 1969, during sessions for *Déjà Vu*, when songs were flowing freely from all of them. This take of 'Do for the Others' is a stunning three-part harmony, acoustic-only rendition of one of the best songs from Stills' first solo album. It would have been a highlight of *Crosby, Stills & Nash* and rightly recognised as a classic Stills original had it been written a few months before.

'Song with No Words (Tree with No Leaves)' (Crosby)

An early Crosby and Nash version of a song later recorded for Crosby's first solo album. This version was recorded on 17 November 1969. Also included on the *CSN* box set.

'Everybody's Talkin'' (Neil)

Also recorded 17 November 1969. This off-the-cuff recording sees this terrific Fred Neil song being given the CSN three-part harmony treatment. It's gorgeous. A version of 'Everybody's Talkin'' performed by Harry Nilsson became a hit in 1969, reaching No. 6 in the US and winning a Grammy Award after it was featured in the film *Midnight Cowboy*. The song's writer, Fred Neil, was a major influence on Stephen Stills. Stills would sing Neil's 'The Dolphins' in later years: there is a stunning version on YouTube, recorded in 2001 as a tribute to Neil who had just died.

'Teach Your Children' (Nash)

An early version of the song later recorded for *Déjà Vu*.

Other contemporary tracks, February-March 1969

'Blackbird' (Lennon/McCartney)

This is CSN's version of The Beatles' song, recorded during sessions for *Crosby, Stills & Nash* on 11 February 1969. Despite being performed in concert many times in 1969, 1970, 1974 and 1977, it wasn't released in any version until the 1983 live album *Allies*. This 1969 outtake is an edit from three separate takes and is available on the *CSN* box set. Other live versions from 1974 and 2012 have been released since.

'You're Wrong Babe' (Nash), **'Why Baby Why'** (Nash)

Two songs supposedly recorded during the February-March 1969 sessions for *Crosby, Stills & Nash*. Engineer Stephen Barncard places these later in 1969 during the *Déjà Vu* sessions. Nash plays a pump organ (or similar) on 'You're Wrong Babe'. 'Why Baby Why' has a copyright date of 11 February 1970. Either way, Nash has not seen fit to release either of these on the *CSN* box set, his own *Reflections* box set or the *Demos* CD.

1970: Déjà Vu

Personnel:
David Crosby: vocals on all tracks except '4+20'; guitar on 'Almost Cut My Hair,' 'Woodstock,' 'Déjà Vu,' 'Country Girl,' and 'Everybody I Love You'
Stephen Stills: vocals all tracks except 'Almost Cut My Hair'; guitars on all tracks except 'Our House'; keyboards on 'Carry On,' 'Helpless,' 'Woodstock,' and 'Déjà Vu'; bass on 'Carry On,' and 'Teach Your Children'; percussion on 'Carry On'
Graham Nash: vocals all tracks except 'Almost Cut My Hair' and '4+20'; keyboards on 'Almost Cut My Hair', 'Woodstock', 'Our House' and 'Everybody I Love You'; guitar on 'Teach Your Children' and 'Country Girl'; percussion on 'Carry On' and 'Teach Your Children'
Neil Young: vocals on 'Helpless' and 'Country Girl'; guitars on 'Almost Cut My Hair', 'Helpless', 'Woodstock', 'Country Girl' and 'Everybody I Love You'; keyboards, harmonica on 'Country Girl'
and
Jerry Garcia: pedal steel guitar on 'Teach Your Children'
Greg Reeves: bass on 'Almost Cut My Hair', 'Helpless', 'Woodstock', 'Déjà Vu', 'Our House', 'Country Girl' and 'Everybody I Love You'
John Sebastian: harmonica on 'Déjà Vu'
Dallas Taylor: drums all tracks except '4+20'; tambourine on 'Teach Your Children'
Recorded Wally Heider's Studio C, July 1969 – January 1970 and at Young's Topanga Canyon studio, January 1970. Produced by Crosby, Stills, Nash and Young.
Produced by Crosby, Stills, Nash & Young.
Released: 11 March 1970 (US). Highest chart positions: 1 (US), 5 (UK).

Crosby, Stills & Nash was released in May 1969 and won a Grammy in 1970 for Best New Artist, with nominations for Album of the Year and Best Contemporary Vocal Performance by a Group.

The single 'Marrakesh Express' followed in July, reaching no. 28 the weekend of the Woodstock festival. With CSN booked to perform at Woodstock, Stills wanted to expand the band to include an electric rhythm section. 'I didn't want us to be another Simon and Garfunkel,' Stills told Dave Zimmer. 'That's what David and Graham were pushing for, but I went 'No, no, no, no!' I mean, the harmonies and the acoustic guitars were part of the show, but not the *whole* show. We needed to rock, too.'

With this decision, the fundamental balance of CSN was disturbed, never quite to settle down again. For the rhythm section, drummer Dallas Taylor was a given. 'A band composed of fairly talented musicians,' he wrote later, 'hampered by enormous egos and the consequent belief that rehearsal was for amateurs.'

Former Buffalo Springfield bassist Bruce Palmer was recruited, but a sixth musician was needed– either a keyboard player or a guitarist. Their original idea was to bring in John B Sebastian, late of the Lovin' Spoonful. Sebastian:

My feelings were very mixed. I loved what they were doing, but I couldn't

> see where I would fit in. I would have been a fourth voice, under theirs, and I would have been playing drums because the last thing they needed was another guitarist. Also I'd just left the Lovin' Spoonful and I'd been lucky to carry over a lot of our fans to my solo career. I really did wonder if I might lose them by throwing in my lot with another new venture. I never actually turned them down. But the idea just kind of eventually just went away.

Steve Winwood, at that time a member of the short-lived Blind Faith, was courted but declined. Mark Naftalin, former keyboard player with the Paul Butterfield Blues Band was also a potential recruit.

The decision to bring in Neil Young cannot have been taken lightly. The Stills-Young dynamic had energised Buffalo Springfield; it had also forced it apart. Initially, Nash was reticent. 'I was against Neil joining at first. I felt a little threatened, because the three of us had made this *thing* of CSN, this album, this sound, and I felt afraid that it was going to change.' Years later, Nash would word this a little differently when interviewed by Debbie Kruger: 'In 1969 when CSN had finished the album, we knew that we would be going on the road. Stephen, as a great lead guitarist, needed someone to 'play-off', to inspire him to play better. Neither David nor I were that person. We play good rhythm guitar, but 'lead' guitar is something different altogether. We decided that we would ask Neil to come along and join the band. At first, I was a little reticent to have this happen. I thought that we had a complete 'band' and a wonderful vocal blend. I spent one morning at breakfast with Neil on Bleeker Street in New York City and when we were finished, I was completely sold on Neil joining. He was incredibly funny and very committed to music. He wanted to be a full member of the band with equal billing etc. This made sense to me and so we became CSNY. Neil's effect on the band was immediate and very fulfilling. He adds a certain edge to the sound and, of course, he is an incredible musician. We became a better band because of the inclusion of Neil Young.' 'I love making music with the guy,' Crosby agrees. 'But he'll do it when he wants to. Because that's how you get the best out of him.'

'I love playing with the other guys,' Young told *Rolling Stone* in 1975, 'but playing with Stephen is special. David is an excellent rhythm guitarist and Graham sings so great... shit, I don't have to tell anybody those guys are phenomenal. I knew it would be fun. I didn't have to be out front. I could lay back. It didn't have to be me all the time. CSNY, I think, has always been a lot bigger thing to everybody else than it is to us. People always refer to me as Neil Young of CSNY, right? It's not my main trip. It's something that I do every once in a while.

'Before I joined Crosby, Stills and Nash, I made it clear to both sides that I belong to myself.' – Neil Young, quoted in *Crosby, Stills and Nash: The Biography*. That quote is very telling. In retrospect, adding Neil Young to CSN was a career-defining, and possibly harmful, decision that has, ever since, resulted in unfair and often damning comparison between Young's work and CSN's. Youngs's second solo album, *Everybody Knows This Is Nowhere*, preceded *Crosby, Stills & Nash* by just two weeks, so Young will have seen his association with CSN as an astute career move. Nevertheless, it seems he deliberately held back some of his best songs of the period for his next solo album, *After the Goldrush*: 'Birds' was performed live by CSNY in 1969, and 'Don't Let It Bring You Down', 'Southern Man', 'Tell Me Why' and 'Only Love Can Break Your Heart' were part of the band's 1970 setlists but never formally recorded by CSNY.

As Alan Pattinson argues:

> [Young's] addition will cast a long shadow over CSNY: at first, because his darker edged vibe and more recalcitrant nature brings such a different feel to this band of brothers and later because he had such a different career to the others, using CSNY as one of many facets of his sound rather than living and breathing it the way the others did.

So, for better or worse, Young was in.

CSNY's 41-date 1969-1970 tour, with the unstable Bruce Palmer replaced by fifteen-year-old Greg Reeves, lasted through January 1970, by which time the follow-up to *Crosby, Stills & Nash* had been completed. Most of the album, *Déjà Vu*, was recorded between October and December 1969; the acoustic despair of '4+20' dates from July 1969.

There's a wider range of moods on *Déjà Vu*. Lacking the consistent tone of the 'Couch Album', *Déjà Vu* is a darker, more tense and more complex album, notwithstanding the catchy singalong pop of 'Our House' and 'Teach Your Children'. It would be nominated for Album of the Year at the 13th Grammy Awards. 'There was a time in late 1970 with *Déjà Vu* at its peak when CSNY were just about the American Beatles. The four of them had clear and separate, slightly adversary identities: Crosby, the former Byrd, the political voice, the California dreamer; Nash, the Briton, the former Hollie, the spiritually hungry searcher; Stills, the guitar hero from Buffalo Springfield; and Young, the brooding dark horse from Canada. They were, at once, steeped in mystique and still the guys next door. – Cameron Crowe, *Rolling Stone*, 1977

Graham Nash has long expressed a desire to remix and re-release this album. 'I'm toying with the idea of redoing *Déjà Vu*,' he said in 2014. 'When we made the album, we were restricted by the technicalities of how many minutes you can get onto a side of vinyl without having to compress everything. It meant we had to fade everything out.' We're still waiting, Graham.

'Carry On' (Stills)

Released as the b-side of 'Teach Your Children', May 1970. Edited remix released as a single, 1980 (did not chart).

A very strong opening song, full of life, with those thrilling Crosby, Stills and

Nash harmonies literally singing out. 'Carry On' is a throwback to *Crosby, Stills & Nash*, with Stills playing bass, organ, percussion, electric guitar and the chiming acoustic guitar (using the Bruce Palmer Modal Tuning once more) and Dallas Taylor on drums. Neil Young does not take part. The second half of the song revisits 'Questions', a Buffalo Springfield song from *Last Time Around*.

'The song was written in the middle of the *Déjà Vu* sessions,' said drummer Dallas Taylor, 'when Nash told Stephen they still didn't have an opener for the album.'

'I was talking to [Stills] one day about the fact that we didn't have an opener for the album,' Nash recalled. 'Like how 'Suite: Judy Blue Eyes' was the opener for the first CSN record. We wanted something that will entice the listener to continue listening. And I told Steve, 'We don't have that.' And he goes, 'Yeah, you're right, let me think about that.' And the very next day he came he said, 'Hey, Willy, listen to this ... ' And he played me 'Carry On.''

'It was something of a message to the group,' says Dallas Taylor, 'Since it had become a real struggle to keep the band together at that point. Stephen combined two unfinished songs and stuck them onto a jam we'd had out in the studio a few nights before, me on drums and Stephen on a Hammond B-3 organ. As the track begins, I'm playing bass drums and high hat, and Graham is playing congas. Then we go into a 6/8 groove, which is rather obscure – Stephen loved to change gears that way.'

An October 1980 remix for the *Replay* compilation removes 'Questions', loops the verses and adds newly-recorded drums and a scintillating Stills electric guitar solo. 'I always wanted to re-cut 'Carry On' without 'Questions',' Stills explains. 'So this seemed the right time to do that. I got Billy Meeker to lay in some new drum tracks and on the second half I cut loose on lead.' A remix of the original track is available on the 2013 box set *Carry On*.

'Teach Your Children' (Nash)

Released as a single, May 1970. B-side 'Carry On'. Highest chart position: 16 (US).

Written whilst Nash was still in the Hollies – hard to believe that they rejected this, 'Marrakesh Express' and 'Lady of the Island'!

'In August of 1968, Graham Nash retired to his room at the Oulton Grove Motel in Leeds, England, after a Hollies gig, lit up some hash and began writing songs. The Hollies had just started work on an album of Bob Dylan covers, and he was desperate to prove to them they should ditch the idea in favour of original compositions. He'd also recently come across the 1962 Diane Arbus photograph *Child with a Toy Hand Grenade in Central Park*, which left him horrified. '[The kid in the photo] had a plastic hand grenade clenched in his fist,' Nash wrote in his 2013 book *Wild Tales: A Rock & Roll Life*, 'but it seemed to me that if it were real the kid would have thrown it. The consequences of it startled me. I thought, 'If we don't start teaching kids a better way of dealing with each other, humanity will never succeed.'' – Andy Greene, *Rolling Stone*, 2018

There are two demos available from February 1969 which reveal this track's origins as a fairly uptight 'slightly funky English folk song'. The earlier of the two is just Nash and his acoustic guitar. The second adds a David Crosby harmony. There are some lyrical differences to the familiar released version; the backing vocal counterpoint has yet to be written. Despite a slight variance in tempo, both are almost identical and may well come from the same session. These can be heard on *Over the Years* and the 2016 CD reissue of *Crosby, Stills & Nash.*

The *Déjà Vu* version was recorded in November 1969. Stills' provided a new arrangement, with hints of Johnny Cash boom-chicka-boom. A counter-point backing vocal was added under the second verse: 'Can you hear and do you care / And can't you see, we must be free / To teach your children / What you believe in / Make a world that we can live in?'

Coupled with Jerry Garcia's first take pedal steel guitar overdub, Nash's universal message resulted in a hugely popular country-tinged pop song which Nash must have played at every concert he's given since 1970. Again. Neil Young does not contribute although he would add his shaky harmonies to subsequent live versions.

'The idea is that you write something so personal that every single person on the planet can relate to it,' Nash said. 'Once it's there on the vinyl it unfolds, outwards, so that it applies to almost any situation. Stephen put a country beat to it and turned it into a hit record.' A subtle alternative mix of 'Teach Your Children' is on *Reflections.* This adds some reverb to the guitars and pushes the vocals a little closer to the front.

We should also add here a 1994 recording by Suzy Boguss, Alison Krauss and Kathy Mattea, with Crosby, Stills and Nash, credited to the Red Hots and released on the album *Red Hot + Country* to raise awareness and money to fight AIDS. This recording was nominated for a Grammy: Best Country Vocal Collaboration.

'Almost Cut My Hair' (Crosby)

Much of David Crosby's work is self-examining and acoustic. But occasionally he gets pissed, as this blast of paranoia attests. 'The whole polarisation of the country was starting to happen,' Crosby later told Dave Zimmer. 'And it had gone from 'Hey, are you a boy or a girl?' to 'Goddamn hippies, let's *kill* 'em all.' That was pretty intense.'

Perfect for the full CNSY electric assault, 'Almost Cut My Hair' features Crosby on electric 12-string, Nash on organ, and Stills and Young on twin lead guitars (left and right channels respectively). Taylor and Reeves are in place on drums and bass. Crosby: 'I wrote 'Almost Cut My Hair' when we were putting ourselves together as a group. We were living in Sag Harbor in an A-frame, which is also where Stephen and Judy Collins finally got together. It's funny it's probably the song I'm most known for, but to me, it's probably my most juvenile, least impressive piece of work. The reason I got so excited about it was because of what Stephen and Neil did with it later.'

In the '80s and '90s, Crosby performed 'Almost Cut My Hair' in a subdued and quiet acoustic arrangement to skin-tingling effect. By 2019: 'I'm a different guy than when I wrote that song, and that guy isn't important to me.'

An unedited take of the *Déjà Vu* version can be heard on the *CSN* box set; an alternative twelve-minute take with three Crosby vocals also exists. An acoustic demo from November 1969 is on the debut album re-issue and the *Voyage* box set; a 2010 live version is included on the album *The 25th Anniversary Rock & Roll Hall of Fame Concerts*.

'Helpless' (Young)

Released as the b-side of 'Woodstock', March 1970.

If the 1-2-3 punch of 'Carry On', 'Teach Your Children' and 'Almost Cut My Hair' doesn't knock you off your seat, then here's the kicker: a perfect, slow, country song recorded, according to Young, 'about four a.m. when everyone got tired enough to play at my speed.' The song's composer plays acoustic guitar, Stills is on piano and electric guitar, Taylor and Reeves on drums and bass, Young sings lead, CSN back him up.

'Woodstock' (Joni Mitchell)

Released as a single, March 1970. B-side 'Helpless'. Highest chart position: 11 (US).

> For a herd of people that large to cooperate so well, it was pretty remarkable and there was tremendous optimism. So I wrote the song 'Woodstock' out of these feelings...
> Joni Mitchell.

Stills' rocking arrangement of Joni Mitchell's paean to three days of peace and love at Max Yasgur's farm. A remarkable version recorded just weeks after the festival, with Stills on organ and vocals, Jimi Hendrix on bass and (I think) Mitch Mitchell on drums, was laid down at the Record Plant in New York on 30 September 1969. This was released in 2018 on the album *Both Sides of the Sky*. Sound engineer Eddie Kramer: 'with Jimi helping the song along, it sounds like Crosby, Stills and Hendrix'.

CSNY's arrangement has Stills singing slightly rearranged lyrics. This puts the line, 'we are billion-year-old carbon' – which only appeared in Joni Mitchell's final chorus – into each of the first three choruses. Then that line was replaced with 'we are caught in the devil's bargain' in the last chorus. CSNY's recording is driven by Stills' organ and Young's lead guitar. Nash plays inaudible piano, Crosby is on electric rhythm. Engineer Russ Gary: 'We recorded 'Woodstock' on a Monday and mixed it that evening [5 November 1969]. Only CS&N and the band were present. We recorded tracks and vocals for 'Teach Your Children' and 'Our House' over the next two days and evenings. Neil Young arrived on Thursday and we recorded the track and vocals for 'Helpless'. CSN&Y's regular recording engineer, Bill Halverson, arrived on Friday and recorded the remainder of the album and mixed it in Studio C at Wally Heider's studio in San Francisco, except for Neil's tracks, which he finished at his own facility.'

''Woodstock' was a great record at first,' Neil Young said in 1975. 'It was a great live record, man. Everyone played and sang at once. Stephen sang the shit out of it. The track was magic. Then, later on, they were in the studio for a long time and started nit-picking. Sure enough, Stephen erased the vocal and put another one on that wasn't nearly as incredible. They did a lot of things over again that I thought were more raw and vital sounding. But that's all personal taste.'

This alternative take has a different lead vocal and less disciplined final guitar break. It can be heard on the *CSN* and *Carry On* box sets. A 2010 live version is included on the album *The 25th Anniversary Rock & Roll Hall of Fame Concerts*. A radically different arrangement by Matthews Southern Comfort was a UK number one single for three weeks in October-November 1970. Joni's version released on *Ladies of the Canyon* three or four weeks after *Déjà Vu* is better than both, but hey.

'Déjà Vu' (Crosby)

Released as the b-side of 'Our House', May 1970.

Crosby's asymmetrical song about reincarnation. 'I remember Nash thinking that 'Déjà Vu' was quite weird,' Crosby recollects, 'which made me very happy. I'm one of those people who thinks we go round again. The Buddhists have got it right – it's a wheel and we get on and get off. I think life energy gets recycled. Lifeforce just doesn't go away. How else can I explain knowing how to sing harmonies at age six or knowing how to sail a boat the first time I got in one? I wasn't thinking about that specifically when I wrote the song. It just came, but in hindsight, the song was informed by those experiences. I felt then and now that I have been here before.'

Crosby's 6 and 12 string acoustic guitars (tuned like 'Guinnevere' to EBDGAD) are embellished by Stills' bass, electric guitar, piano and acoustic piano. Nash adds harmonies and John B Sebastian provides harmonica. Neil Young is absent once more.

Two (different) demos from November 1969 can be heard on the *Voyage* box set and the *Demos* album. Intriguingly *Rolling Stone*'s 5 April 1969 issue lists 'Déjà Vu' as due for release on CSN's debut album, in place of 'Long Time Gone'.

'Our House' (Nash)

Released as a single, May 1970. B-side 'Déjà Vu'. Highest chart position: 30 (US).

Graham Nash was never afraid to wear his heart on his sleeve, even when the results headed towards mawkishness. Nash sings (brilliantly, it must be said) and plays everything here other than bass, drums and backing vocals. It's a popular song, but would you worry if you never heard it again?

'[This song originated with] me and Joni going to breakfast and passing an antiques store on the way home and it was terribly cold – a foggy rainy Los Angeles morning. Just awful. We got back to Joni's house and I said, 'Hey, why don't I light a fire and you put some flowers in that vase you just bought?''

The song was written on the same piano as Mitchell's 'Rainy Night House', 'Ladies of the Canyon' and 'Morning Morgantown'. Her quite brilliant 'River' depicts her breakup with Nash in 1970: 'I'm so hard to handle, I'm selfish and I'm sad. / Now I've gone and lost the best baby that I've ever had. / Oh, I wish I had a river I could skate away on.' Sigh.

A demo version of 'Our House' recorded at Wally Heider Recording, Hollywood in November 1969, was released in 2018 on *Over the Years*.

'4 + 20' (Stills)

Another odd guitar tuning here: DADDAD. The deft fingerpicking, ringing strings and Stills' exposed, unembellished vocals (hear him catch his breath at 1:42) give '4 +20' a rare vulnerability and freshness not usually associated with his often bullish persona. Stills encapsulates deep feelings of melancholia in only 120 seconds.

'I wanted to hold it for my solo album,' Stills notes, 'but the guys insisted we use it on *Déjà Vu* – it means a lot to me – it's about an eighty-four-year-old, poverty-stricken man who started and finished with nothing. I recorded the track in one take. I'd intended for David and Graham to sing harmony and even had the parts worked out, but they told me they wouldn't dare touch it, so it always stood alone.'

Neil Young must have been green with envy.

A remix with a touch more reverb is available on the *CSN* and *Carry On* box sets. CSN did, indeed, sometimes perform this in three-part harmony, notably in their *MTV Unplugged* broadcast in 1990.

'Country Girl (Whiskey Boot Hill, Down Down Down, Country Girl (I Think You're Pretty)' (Young)

An astounding song – not so far from 'Broken Arrow' and 'Expecting to Fly' from Young's Buffalo Springfield days, but with added intensity. Performed during Young's contemporary solo shows and in a handful of CSNY shows in 1969-1970, the studio arrangement takes some outrageous chords and full band harmonies, combining these with Young's majestic organ and shimmering electric piano, Stills' piano trills and Dallas Taylor's booming tympani to majestic effect.

The song's title appears to come from a Clifford Odets play *The Country Girl*, performed by the Topanga Canyon Playhouse Company in 1966 and featuring Young's future wife Susan Acevedo. Young remembers, 'I used to go to the Canyon Kitchen every morning for breakfast. Susan Acevedo, the beautiful Sicilian hostess/owner, would bring me a one-eye and bacon. I got to look at

Susan Acevedo every day at breakfast!' They married on 1 December 1968.

Parts of 'Country Girl' were recorded at Young's own studio, without the rest of the band. 'I was a little resentful of Neil taking his tracks out of the studio,' Nash commented later. 'I was a junkie for music, and I wanted to be there to see all of those overdubs go down. But with Neil's stuff, I loved the end result. When I heard 'Country Girl', what could I say? There was no point in getting uptight because it was beautiful.'

Stephen Stills must have been green with envy.

'Everybody I Love You' (Stills / Young)

The album ends with Stills' short, intense 'Everybody I Love You', pieced together from two earlier songs: 'You Can Dance Really Good' and 'Every Day We Live'. 'Neil had a riff,' Stills recalled in 1970, 'and I had a seven-minute track of another song we've done at my house. We took bits and pieces and put them all together.' Stills plays piano, organ and lead guitar against Young's second lead part, and Crosby's rhythm. There are only four confirmed live performances of this song. It is, by some distance, the least-performed song from the band's first two albums.

Other contemporary tracks, June-December 1969

'Bluebird Revisited' (Stills)

Recorded at Sunwest Studios, LA, on 17 June 1969 and at Wally Heider's in October 1969 (these versions remain unreleased). Performed live during the band's 1969 dates. Re-recorded for *Stephen Stills 2*.

'Cinnamon Girl' (Young)

An instrumental CSNY studio run-through of one of Young's most powerful songs, with Stills on organ.

'Down by the River' (Young)

A Neil Young song from *Everybody Knows This Is Nowhere*, never formally recorded by CSNY but performed live in 1969. The scintillating version seen in the film *Celebration at Big Sur*, recorded mid-September 1969, shows you why these four men have constantly tried to re-create the magic of that first tour.

'Everybody's Alone' (Young)

Part of CSNY's October 1969 sessions at the Record Plant in LA. A contemporary Neil Young / Crazy Horse recording can be heard on *Archives Vol. 1*. An earlier Young solo demo has been circulating for years.

'Everybody's Been Burned' (Crosby)

This is a Graham Nash solo demo from August 1970 during the first sessions for *Songs for Beginners*, so strictly outside the scope of the *Déjà Vu* sessions.

It's included in several CSNY sessions bootleg albums (and is very good), so we include it here for completeness. Yes, Graham Nash sings one of Crosby's songs from early 1967.

'['Everybody's Been Burned'] was probably the first good song that I wrote,' Crosby recalled in 2011. 'I'd written other songs before that, but I think that was probably the first *good* one. Graham sings it as well I do.' 'I love that song,' Nash agrees. 'It was brilliantly constructed. It really touched my heart because, when you think about it, *everybody's* been burned in some way at some point.'

'Horses Through a Rainstorm' (Nash / Reid)

Graham Nash met Terry Reid at the Royal Albert Hall in London when the band that Reid performed in, the Jaywalkers, was a support act for the Rolling Stones. Reid's song 'Without Expression', from his debut solo album, was recorded by The Hollies in 1968 as 'A Man with No Expression'. Rewritten by Nash as 'Horses Through a Rainstorm', it was presented by Nash to CSNY and recorded on 28 December 1969. This terrific outtake was released on the *CSN* box set in 1991. Greg Reeves: 'There was a song that Graham wrote I thought should have been on the LP which was called 'Horses Through a Rainstorm'. Great song by Graham.'

It's a knock-out track, sounding half-way between the Hollies and the first Crosby-Nash album, driven by Stills' powerful organ and with a classic late 60s middle-eight. Nash's solo demo from Autumn 1968 is available on *Over the Years* (2018).

The song was also recorded by REO Speedwagon in 1973 as 'Without Expression (Don't Be the Man)'.

'How Have You Been?' (Sebastian)

A song from John B Sebastian's 1970 self-titled solo album, CSN's version from November 1969, nothing more than a run-through but full of spirit, was first released in 1991 on the compilation album *Nintendo: White Knuckle Scorin'*. One assumes it was a candidate for the band's expansive box set released that same year. The song was performed a few times during acoustic sets in late 1969.

'The Lee Shore' (Crosby)

A beautiful song, foreshadowing the Crosby / Nash collaborations of the 1970s.

The first released version is on the 1971 live album *4 Way Street*. Two studio takes have surfaced since: the earliest was recorded on 15 July 1969, sung by Stephen Stills with his favourite Latin rhythms and it is on the *Carry On* box set. A full band run through from the *Déjà Vu* sessions (28 December 1969 with 1991 vocal overdubs) is on the *CSN* box set. The pre-overdubs take circulates on bootleg.

'I wrote 'Lee Shore' on the Mayan in the Berry Islands in the Bahamas,' Crosby recalls. 'In hindsight, I love sailing because it was a thing that kept me in touch with the real world. It's not just drugs that keep you from the real world; fame does, money does. If you buy into those things, the real world goes away. On the boat, you either have your shit together or you don't. The ocean doesn't know who you are. Couldn't care less.'

'Right Between the Eyes' (Nash)

One of many songs written by Nash during this period. 'I was seduced by a beautiful woman down in Long Island,' Nash told Rolling Stone in 2009. 'She was married. The song is a confession to a friend.' That friend was John B Sebastian.

'Right Between the Eyes' was a candidate for *Déjà Vu*: a demo version had been recorded at Wally Heider Recording, Hollywood, in November 1969 and this is available on Nash's *Reflections* (2009) and *Over the Years* (2018). A live version can be heard on *4 Way Street*.

'Same Old Song' (Stills)

From a CSNY rehearsal at Sunwest Studios, LA, 15 June 1969.

'Sea of Madness' (Young)

Part of CSNY's electric set in 1969 and recorded 13/15 July 1969 at Stephen Stills' house, this is now available on *Archives Vol 1*. A live version from September 1969 at the Fillmore East in New York was used on the *Woodstock* soundtrack album and there is a better version in the *Celebration at Big Sur* documentary film, also recorded September 1969. It's a fun rocker, with Young's aggressive vocal tempered by Crosby and Nash's backing vocals. Stills on lead, Young on organ.

'So Begins the Task' (Stills)

One of Stills' best songs, first recorded at the 1968 sessions that gave us *Just Roll Tape* in 2007. It was recorded by CSNY at Sunwest Studios, LA, on 17 June 1969– this remains unreleased– and was performed live during the band's 1969 concert dates. Studio recordings of this exquisite song can be heard on *Manassas* (1972) and *Everybody Knows* (2017). Stephen Stills: 'I thought of this song as a poem. It was written immediately after 'Helplessly Hoping'. It's a song of loss but also the freedom that goes with loss.'

'Triad' (Crosby)

Crosby's version of the song that had him kicked out of the Byrds. His acoustic demo was recorded 17 November 1969 and now available on the *Voyage* box set. A live version is a highlight of *4 Way Street*. The Byrds' version from August 1967 remained unreleased until 1987. Crosby also gave the song to Jefferson Airplane who included it on *Crown of Creation*, recorded in May 1968.

'You Can Dance Really Good', '$30 Fine', 'Master My Fear', 'She Can't Handle It', 'Whole People', 'Ivory Tower', 'Everyday We Live'(all Stills)

Seven Stills songs recorded at his house in June-July 1969. Other than 'Every Day We Live' which is an upbeat Stills pop song with Young's guitar to the fore and Nash pounding the organ, the rest may or may not be CSNY outtakes, and they may or not have been intended for a solo project. Either way, the recordings exist and are included here as possible CSNY sessions. Both '$30 Fine' and 'Ivory Tower' formed part of sessions at the Record Plant, LA, in October 1969 and sessions at Wally Heider's the following month. 'Ivory Tower' was rewritten as 'Sugar Babe' on *Stephen Stills 2*. '$30 Fine', renamed '$20 Fine', was released by Jimi Hendrix on the album *Both Sides of the Sky* in 2018: Stills plays organ, the recording date is 30 September 1969.

'You've Got to Hide Your Love Away' (Lennon / McCartney)

Recorded in November 1969. Never heard.

Non-Album single

'Ohio' (Young)

Released as a single, June 1970. B-side 'Find the Cost of Freedom'. Highest chart position: 14 (US).

The Kent State shootings shocked liberal America. On 4 May 1970, twenty-eight National Guard soldiers fired approximately 67 rounds at unarmed college students who were protesting at Kent State in Ohio, killing four, paralysing one and wounding eight others. Astonishingly, future world-famous musicians Chrissie Hynde (The Pretenders), Joe Walsh (Eagles) and Bob Lewis and Gerald Casale (Devo) were present that day. Chrissie Hynde was eighteen years old at the time and recalls: 'The grassy, rolling common was teeming with students, I'd never seen it so packed… Then I heard the 'tatatatatatatatatat' sound. I thought it was fireworks. An eerie silence fell over the common. Then a young man's voice: 'They fucking killed somebody.''

Life magazine covered the Kent State shootings in detail in their 15 May issue, headlined 'Tragedy at Kent': 'The upheaval in Kent seemed at its outset to be merely another of the scores of student demonstrations that have rocked U.S. campuses. But before it ended, in senseless and brutal murder at point-blank range, Kent State had become a symbol of the fearful hazards latent in dissent, and in the policies that cause it.'

'The way I recall it,' says David Crosby, 'I was with Neil at a friend's house and handed him *Life* magazine with the Kent State photos. He was silent for a long time, then picked up his guitar and twenty minutes later had this song. I called Stephen and Graham, and we immediately booked a studio.'

Engineer Bill Halverson says: 'I'm at the studio setting up for [a] session and

I got a call from, I think, one of the roadies that was over at the sound stage and he said there's been a change in plans and the band's got this song that they wanna do together and so set up for the whole band; we're all gonna come out. They're rehearsing it right now. They're going to come on in a couple of hours and we're going to record it.'

'We gave the master to Ahmet Ertegun,' Crosby says, 'who flew it to New York the next day and it was released within the week.'

Acetates were rushed to major radio stations, even though 'Teach Your Children' was already on the charts at the time. Within two and a half weeks of the Kent State shootings, 'Ohio'– a very angry song– was receiving national airplay. Crosby: ''Teach Your Children' was heading straight for number one, and we knocked it right off the charts with our own song, and Nash never said one word about it, to his great credit. He knew how important it was that this song be out there. For me 'Ohio' was a high point of the band, a major point of validity. There we were, reacting to reality, dealing with it on the highest level we could – relevant, immediate. It named names and pointed the finger.'

Neil Young: 'It's still hard to believe I had to write this song. It's ironic that I capitalised on the death of these American students. Probably the most important lesson ever learned at an American place of learning. David Crosby cried after this take.'

The song was first performed live on 29 May 1970 in Boston. They would perform it in Cleveland, Ohio on 3 July 1970. Lorne Keegan, a student at Kent State, later recalled that performance: 'People were on their feet, you know, clapping their hands, moving their bodies, crying. Everybody was sort of shaking ... You listen to the music now and it seems so candyish. Then it seemed to have a purpose.'

In 2011 'Ohio' was listed as the 385th greatest song of all time by *Rolling Stone*. A longer version, 4:06 in length, circulates amongst collectors – the quality is horrible, but it does come to a natural end without fading.

'Find the Cost of Freedom' (Stills)

Released as the b-side of 'Ohio', June 1970.

The pure essence of Crosby, Stills, Nash and Young – just acoustic guitars and four voices.

'I wrote it at the request of Dennis Hopper for the final scene in *Easy Rider*,' says Stephen Stills, 'where the dude gets blown away as his motorcycle burns and the camera pans way up in the sky. I played it for Dennis, but he was in a fog and just didn't get it. We ended every CSNY concert with this song. After a long evening and raucous electric set, we'd come back out with acoustic guitars, sit quietly on stools, and play this song. Leave everybody in a quiet space together.'

'I went out and set up four chairs so they'd be facing each other' recalls engineer Bill Halverson, 'And set up four vocal mics and a guitar mic. They sat knee to knee and sang it through. I rewound the tape and rolled it again, and Stephen played along with himself, a little on guitar, played the little fills and stuff…'

The song is played in Double Drop D tuning – DADGBD.

1971: 4 Way Street

Personnel:
David Crosby: vocals, guitar
Stephen Stills: vocals, guitar, piano, organ
Graham Nash: vocals, guitar, piano, organ
Neil Young: vocals, guitar
and
Johnny Barbata: drums on 'Pre-Road Downs', 'Long Time Gone', 'Southern Man', 'Ohio' and 'Carry On'
Calvin 'Fuzzy' Samuel: bass on 'Pre-Road Downs', 'Long Time Gone', 'Southern Man', 'Ohio' and 'Carry On'
Recorded June and July 1970 on CSNY's US tour. Produced by Crosby, Stills, Nash & Young.
Released 7 April 1971 (US). Highest chart positions: 1 (US), 5 (UK).

After completing *Déjà Vu* in January 1970, Stephen Stills recorded his first solo album, *Stephen Stills*, in London and Los Angeles, and Neil Young completed his third, *After the Goldrush*, in Topanga. Both albums were released in November 1970. CSNY re-convened for twenty-four live dates between May and July 1970. A live album documenting the tour, *4 Way Street,* would follow in April 1971, bookended by David Crosby's *If I Could Only Remember My Name* (recorded August-November 1970, released February 1971) and Graham Nash's *Songs for Beginners* (mostly recorded January-February 1971, released May 1971).

The album is a faithful representation of a typical CSNY show, but with lots of the between-song chatter edited out. In addition to songs from *Crosby, Stills & Nash*, *Déjà Vu*, and both sides of their current single they add selections from their soon-to-be-released solo albums, some new songs ('The Lee Shore' and 'Right Between the Eyes'), and some songs first recorded by the Byrds ('Triad') and Buffalo Springfield ('On the Way Home' and 'For What It's Worth'– the latter renamed 'America's Children' and with a hilarious stoner rap rant from Stills). The CD re-release adds a further four songs.

The majority of *4 Way Street* comes from two shows at the Chicago Auditorium on 5/6 July 1970– almost the last dates of the tour.

Known recording dates are:
2 June, Fillmore East, New York: 'Pre-Road Downs'
5 June, Fillmore East, New York: 'Laughing'
6 June, Fillmore East, New York: 'King Midas in Reverse', 'Ohio'
7 June, Fillmore East, New York: 'Find the Cost of Freedom', 'Black Queen', 'The Loner / Cinnamon Girl / Down by the River'
28 June: 'Carry On' (second part)
5 July, Chicago Auditorium: 'Chicago', 'Cowgirl in the Sand', 'Don't Let It Bring You Down', 'Carry On' (first part)
6 July, Chicago Auditorium: 'On the Way Home', 'Teach Your Children', 'Right

Between the Eyes', '49 Bye-Byes / America's Children', 'Southern Man'

Recording dates are not confirmed for 'Suite: Judy Blue Eyes', 'Triad', 'The Lee Shore', 'Love the One You're With' or 'Long Time Gone' but they are certainly taken from this series of shows. The CD version has been brilliantly remastered: it sounds like you're on stage with CSNY in 1970.

'Suite: Judy Blue Eyes' (Stills)

A thirty-second tease, with Neil Young off-stage. Imagine having the balls to open your set with this! It's just the final part of the song, after which the audience quite rightly goes nuts. CSN would often perform 'Blackbird' at this point before introducing 'our friend Neil Young'.

'On the Way Home' (Young)

A Buffalo Springfield song from *Last Time Around*, sung there by Richie Furay but here skilfully reworked as a two-guitar, four-voice acoustic song, fitting right into the singer-songwriter milieu of 1970. Stills' fluid guitar soloing is a highlight. CSNY never sounded more together than during this performance. When they hit it, they were better than anyone.

'Teach Your Children' (Nash)

'Teach Your Children' had been released as a single just a few weeks before this 6 July recording, and was heading up the charts to its peak of #16 a couple of weeks later. There's some applause as the song begins, but at this stage, the audience seem merely pleased to hear 'Teach Your Children'. It's place in the CSNY pantheon was yet to come.

'Triad' (Crosby)

Nash: 'I'm not sure what sort of mood our David's in, but whatever happens is gonna be ah... whatever happens. Few words of wisdom there!' Crosby: 'Sheer profundity. I guess we're never sure what mood we're gonna be in, ever. I got a song and I wanna sing it. I sing it a lot. I don't know, tonight's weird. I'll probably sing it anyway. We have a lot of trouble with that, 'cos we write a lot of our songs just right out of what goes on, you know, to us and about people that we love and stuff and things that happen to us, you know, 'cos like that's what you have to write about if you gonna get down to stuff that means anything to you. So sometimes it's really hard to sing them too. It's also groovy to do it anyway.'

And Crosby delivers an atmospheric, tender, solo acoustic masterpiece. Don't listen to the words too hard, but enjoy the raw emotion and wide-open performance.

'The Lee Shore' (Crosby)

The first release for this song: four other versions have since been made available by Stills, CSNY and Crosby & Nash. Crosby meditates on the joys of sailing.

'Chicago' (Nash)

Nash's first overtly political song. Many more would follow. The title refers to anti-Vietnam War protests that took place during the 1968 Democratic National Convention in Chicago and the subsequent trial of the protest leaders who were charged with conspiracy to incite a riot. The first line ('So your brother's bound and gagged, and they've chained him to a chair') refers to Black Panther leader Bobby Seale who was restrained and tied to a chair in the courtroom following repeated outbursts in protest of rulings by Judge Julius Hoffman. Nash dedicates the song to Richard J Daley, Chicago's major from 1955 to 1976 who was notoriously antagonistic towards anti-war protesters. Nash makes up for his lack of skill on the piano with a spirited performance which the Chicago crowd laps up.

'Right Between the Eyes' (Nash)

'Right Between the Eyes' starts with a mistake, presumably spontaneous, when Crosby sings the wrong words to Nash's new song.

> Crosby: 'This is a song that you had not heard, of Graham Nash's.'
> Nash [sings]: 'My head is...'
> Crosby: 'Sorry, man! I didn't… I could never have believed that you'd have tuned and started on the same note, but you could do it!'
> Nash: 'I couldn't believe it either!'
> Crosby: 'Ha! Whoo! He's quicker than most normal human beings, and sometimes I forget. He's very quick. You don't want to play mumblety-peg with him, he'll steal your leg!'
> Nash: 'This is a song about changes everyone else, y'know, goes through at the same time.'

What follows is a simple Nash confessional song, with a fine, wordless vocal duet between Nash and Crosby not so dissimilar to 'Lady of the Island'.

'Cowgirl in the Sand' (Young)

A radical re-working of the ten-minute guitar wig-out from *Everybody Knows This is Nowhere*, now re-cast as a hugely effective acoustic song, mesmerising and powerful. Young has the audience in the palm of his hands after this scintillating performance.

'Don't Let It Bring You Down' (Young)

An as-then unreleased song from the forthcoming *After the Goldrush*, so unfamiliar to this Chicago audience. Young detunes his low E string and declares 'Here's a new song; it's guaranteed to bring you right down… it's called 'Don't Let It Bring You Down'… sorta starts out real slow and then it fizzles out altogether.'

It's perfection in song.

'49 Bye-Byes/America's Children' (Stills)

Stills attacks his piano in this medley of '49 Reasons' (sic) and 'For What It's Worth' (sic). He adds a hilarious rant which might have ended the career of lesser artists: 'Well it looks to me like there's a few politicians hanging around children. Perpetrating some kind of myth on us all. All right. Taking 'bout what a drag all the kids are, yeah! 'Cause they got the guts to get out in the streets and tell the truth every day. Aahh yes! Making it a little hot for them, you know? All right! But you know that we're all just out there proving to Richard Nixon and Spiro Agnew and Richard Daley and all them other, well whatever you want to call them, that America is still the home of the brave! Oh yes, it is! And you got to be brave children. How many is it that they shot down already? Something like seventeen of us. But you know we gotta do it. We gotta keep on keeping on. Because if we don't do it nobody else is gonna. But you know if we can't do it with a smile on our face… You know if we can't love in our hearts then children we ain't got no right to do it at all. Because it just means we ain't learned nothing yet. We're supposed to be some kind of different. Ahhh! Whoa! Whoa! Whoa! Oh yes! And I don't know if I want white America to remember or to forget that Jesus Christ was the first non-violent revolutionary. Dig it! Ohh! Dig it! Ooh! Right on! Dig it! Yeah!'

'Love the One You're With' (Stills)

Yes, there was a time when audiences heard this warhorse for the first time. After 1970 Stills would perform this song in a horrible electric and decidedly unsubtle arrangement. This acoustic take is as charming as it is ragged and something of a relief after the bombast of the previous track.

'Pre-Road Downs' (Nash)

A straightforward, fast, tight rendition of Nash's rocker from *Crosby, Stills & Nash*: a good opener to the electric set. The rhythm session really cooks and Stills' lead guitar soars above everything. Young is on organ.

'Long Time Gone' (Crosby)

The best version of 'Long Time Gone' will always be the powerful, almost desperate, studio recording on *Crosby, Stills & Nash*. Crosby doesn't quite reach that intensity here, but Fuzzy Samuel's bassline is busier and better than the studio version and combines effectively with Johnny Barbata's thumping drums. Stills on organ, Young on lead guitar.

'Southern Man' (Young)

An intense thirteen-minute version of one of the key tracks in Neil Young's entire discography. As Young says, 'this is usually a really long song, folks, and we're going to do it real slow tonight'. Once again kudos must go to the Samuel / Barbata rhythm section who underpin the seemingly endless soloing from Stills (left) and Young (right). Nash on organ.

'Ohio' (Young)
CSNY's 'Ohio' single was the single was released in June 1970, very close to the performance date of this dazzling live version of Young's most important CSNY song.

'Carry On' (Stills)
A hoarse-voiced, loud, unsubtle electric take of 'Carry On' that lasts for thirteen prolonged minutes. Almost ten of these comprise long, long guitar solos from Stills, wah-wah pedal in overdrive, and Young, wide-open and narrow at the same time. This flaccid version of 'Carry On' challenges the listener to stay through to the end. It is edited from two different performances.

'Find the Cost of Freedom' (Stills)
A return to 'Wooden music' as Crosby would have it. It takes a while for the crowd to calm down, but with Stills and Young on acoustics guitars and all four on vocals this is very similar to the studio version.

1992 bonus tracks

'King Midas In Reverse' (Nash / Clarke / Hicks)
A Nash solo acoustic rendition of the ambitious Hollies single from September 1967. Nash's voice is exposed, but it's an intimate and accomplished performance, nevertheless.

'Laughing' (Crosby)
Unreleased at the time, this stripped-down solo performance is a long way from the magnificence of the studio track recorded later that year. It's still quite astonishing though.

'Black Queen' (Stills)
A country blues: one listen to this confirms Stills' significant capacity as a guitarist and singer. This is the recording when someone in the Fillmore East crowd laughs and Stills stops playing and grunts 'one thing the blues ain't is funny'. And then tears the house down. This same recording is included on the *CSN* box set.

'Medley: The Loner/Cinnamon Girl/Down by the River' (Young)
Not so much a medley as three songs performed in sequence. 'The Loner' is a highlight from Young's first solo album, heard here in an effective acoustic arrangement. The transition to 'Cinnamon Girl', one of Young's stone-cold classics, is supremely effective: a goosebump moment. The abrupt key change and decrease in tempo to 'Down by the River' are less successful – this last-named doesn't translate to the acoustic setting quite so well despite a cheer of recognition from the New York crowd. Young's guitar is slightly out-of-tune and this combines with his trademark shaky vocals to devastating effect.

Other live tracks: 1969-1970

Several complete CSNY concerts were professionally recorded in 1969 and 1970, including those at Woodstock (18 August 1969), Big Sur (13-14 September), Fillmore East, New York (19-20 September), three in December 1969 (dates and venues unconfirmed), Fillmore East, New York (6 concerts, 2-7 June 1970), the Forum, Los Angeles (26 and 28 June 1970), and Chicago Auditorium (5-6 July 1970). The three complete concerts from 4, 5 and 6 June circulate amongst collectors in very good quality. There is also, thrillingly, some high-quality footage of the Fillmore dates in Young's film *Journey Through the Past*. I urge you to track this down on YouTube.

The double album *Woodstock: Music from the Original Soundtrack and More*, released in May 1970 includes versions of 'Suite: Judy Blue Eyes' and 'Wooden Ships' from the concert, along with a live take of Neil Young's 'Sea of Madness', recorded 20 September 1969 at the Fillmore East in New York. CSNY's coming out party. *Woodstock Two*, released July 1971, adds 'Guinnevere', '4+20' and 'Marrakesh Express'.

To mark the concert's 25th anniversary in 1994, these same six tracks were re-released on a four-CD set called *Woodstock: Three Days of Peace and Music* with an additional track: 'Find the Cost of Freedom'. 'Blackbird' was made available on a companion album called *Woodstock Diary*.

The 40th anniversary 6 CD set from 2009, *Woodstock 40 Years On: Back to Yasgur's Farm*, re-issues the songs from the first two albums, but replaces the rogue 'Sea of Madness' with the performance from Woodstock.

Finally, to mark the event's fiftieth anniversary, an immense re-issue called *Woodstock – Back to the Garden: The Definitive 50th Anniversary Archive* collected almost the complete performances by every artist involved. CSNY's complete set, disc 33 of 38, includes 'Suite: Judy Blue Eyes', 'Blackbird', 'Helplessly Hoping', 'Guinnevere', 'Marrakesh Express', '4 + 20', 'Mr. Soul', 'Wonderin'', 'You Don't Have to Cry', 'Pre-Road Downs', 'Long Time Gone', 'Bluebird Revisited', 'Sea of Madness', 'Wooden Ships', 'Find the Cost of Freedom' and '49 Bye-Byes'.

A CSNY version of Neil Young's 'I've Loved Her So Long', recorded live in 1969, was included on the vast *Archives Volume 1* box set (2009).

A few rarities from CSNY's June / July 1970 tour have appeared. 'Find the Cost of Freedom' and 'Southern Man' from the Fillmore East, 5 June 1970 can be found on Neil Young's *Journey Thru the Past* (1972). Nash's 'Man in the Mirror' from the Fillmore East, 2 June 1970, is included on the *CSN* box set (1991). Young's 'Tell Me Why' (gorgeous) and 'Only Love Can Break Your Heart', most probably from New York in June 1970, were included on *Archives Volume 1* (2009).

Another 1970 recording of 'Find the Cost of Freedom' is on the Stephen Stills retrospective box set *Carry On* (2013).

1977: CSN

Personnel:
David Crosby: vocals; rhythm guitar on 'Fair Game' and 'Dark Star'; acoustic guitar on 'Just A Song Before I Go' and 'In My Dreams'
Stephen Stills: vocals; guitars on all tracks except 'Carried Away,' 'Cathedral' and 'Cold Rain'; electric piano on 'Anything at All'; timbales on 'Fair Game'
Graham Nash: vocals; piano on 'Carried Away,' 'Cathedral,' 'Just A Song Before I Go,' and 'Cold Rain'; harmonica on 'Carried Away'
and
Ray Barretto: congas on 'Fair Game'
Craig Doerge: piano on 'Shadow Captain' and 'Anything at All'; electric piano on 'Shadow Captain' and 'Dark Star'
Tim Drummond: bass on 'Just A Song Before I Go'
Mike Finnigan: organ on 'Run from Tears'
Jimmy Haslip: bass on 'Carried Away'
Gerald Johnson: bass on 'Run from Tears'
Russ Kunkel: drums on 'Shadow Captain', 'Anything at All', 'Just A Song Before I Go', and 'In My Dreams'; congas on 'Shadow Captain', 'Dark Star'; percussion on 'Just A Song Before I Go'
George 'Chocolate' Perry: bass on 'Shadow Captain', 'Fair Game', 'Anything at All', 'Cathedral', 'Dark Star' and 'I Give You Give Blind'
Joe Vitale: drums on 'Carried Away', 'Fair Game', 'Cathedral', 'Dark Star', 'Run From Tears' and 'I Give You Give Blind'; organ on 'Shadow Captain', 'Fair Game', 'Anything at All', 'Dark Star'; electric piano on 'Carried Away', 'Just A Song Before I Go'; percussion on 'Cathedral', 'I Give You Give Blind'; flute on 'Shadow Captain'; timpani on 'Cathedral'; vibraphone on 'In My Dreams'
Recorded December 1976 – January 1977 at the Record Plant, LA, and Criteria Studios, Miami. Produced by Crosby, Stills and Nash with Ron and Howard Albert.
Released: 17 June 1977 (US). Highest chart position: 2 (US), 23 (UK).

> '[Crosby, Stills & Nash] always had that Judy Garland, tragic American hero aura about them,' a former business associate remembers. 'It's still going on. Were they strong enough to survive? Would they kill each other? Did they really like their audience? Were they leaders? Was it all for the bucks? Would they fall apart before reaching the top?'
> *Rolling Stone*, 2 June 1977

Crosby, Stills, Nash and Young reunited briefly in 1972 and 1973, undertook a summer-long tour in 1974 and completed further inconclusive recording sessions as 1974 turned into 1975.

Crosby and Nash were invited to Miami to join Stills and Young for recording sessions in April 1976. These, once again, ended in acrimony.

'Just when it seemed things were rolling along,' Nash wrote in his memoirs, 'All the old demons rose up to embrace us. To make matters worse, when Croz and I went back to LA, with every intention of returning to Miami, I heard that Neil and Stephen had come up with the brilliant idea to take David's and my vocals off the tracks and turn it into a Stills/Young record. When word of it got back to us, we totally flipped out. I couldn't believe anyone would be crass enough to wipe our voices off those tracks, and, if true, it was disrespectful to us and, much worse, to the music. All of our good work unheard and wasted. Just completely wrong and unjustifiable. I swore I would never work with them again.'

Hatchets must have been quickly buried. Perhaps the humiliating failure of the Stills-Young Band tour (June-July 1976) prompted Stills to contrition? Or did his divorce from his French singer wife Véronique Sanson push him back to former partners?

Whatever the reason(s), Stills showed up backstage, uninvited, at a Crosby / Nash show at the Greek Theatre in LA on 11 August 1976. Nash:

> It was good to see him. I hugged him. And it amazed me. 'Cause I realised in the middle of the hug that the last time we'd met he'd wiped some very valuable work of David's and mine ... but it didn't matter. We're all incredibly changeable people, God knows, and Stephen had come with his hat in his hand. So fuck it. I hugged him.

Crosby:

> After that last debacle, I looked at Nash like he'd lost his total mind. I thought he was just out of his fucking tree. Completely. Then I hugged Stills too ... the pencil-neck wimp.

They sang 'Teach Your Children' as the encore, got drunk at Nash's place and decided to reunite as a trio. The first songs for the second CSN album were laid down before Christmas: 'Carried Away' and 'Just a Song Before I Go', both by Nash, were the foundation for a more mature, much smoother album than *Crosby, Stills & Nash* or *Déjà Vu*. They revisited 'See the Changes' from the aborted 1973 CSNY sessions. Crosby provided three of his strongest songs. Most of the new Stills songs were his best for several years. And Nash was still at his songwriting peak: the artistic dark horse of Crosby, Stills and Nash.

CSN was co-produced by Ron and Howard Albert, who had worked with Stills on *Manassas*, *Down the Road*, *Stills* and *Illegal Stills*. They had engineered *Layla and Other Assorted Love Songs* and Brook Benton's 'Rainy Night in Georgia' in 1970.The mid-70s AOR feel was achieved by deft employment of some long term sessioners/live band musicians, including Russ Kunkel, Stills' solo band drummer since1974; Chocolate Perry, Stills' solo band bassist since 1975; Joe Vitale, drummer and/or keyboard player for Stills for decades, also working with the Eagles and Joe Walsh; and especially Craig Doerge, Crosby and Nash's piano player and occasional co-composer whose lyrical jazz-tinged piano playing on 'Shadow Captain' and 'Anything at All' adds much to the musical colour on this cleanly produced album.

So, the songs are strong, the performances spirited, the production uncluttered and slick. *CSN* would become the trio's best-selling album, sticking at no. 2 behind the ubiquitous *Rumours*. It was all but ignored in the UK's summer of punk.

Crosby, Stills and Nash would tour extensively in June, October and November 1977. Opening with an electric set, a typical CSN concert of this period would include 'Pre-Road Downs', 'Love the One You're With', 'The Lee Shore', 'I Used to Be a King', 'Dark Star', 'Just a Song Before I Go', 'Shadow Captain', 'Turn Back the Pages' and 'Long Time Gone'. A strong acoustic set featured 'Suite: Judy Blue Eyes', 'You Don't Have to Cry', 'Guinnevere', 'Our House', 'Cathedral', 'Crossroads'/'You Can't Catch Me', 'Helplessly Hoping', 'Blackbird', 'Carry Me' and 'To The Last Whale…'. The full band would take it home with 'Military Madness', 'I Give You Give Blind', 'Run From Tears', 'Déjà Vu', and 'Carry On', with encores of 'Wooden Ships', 'Teach Your Children' and 'Find the Cost of Freedom'. CSN would be nominated for Best Pop Vocal Performance by a Group at the 20th Grammy Awards in 1978.

Crosby, Stills and Nash, older, wiser and now in their mid-thirties, were back on top. Neil who?

'Shadow Captain' (Crosby / Doerge)

Released as the b-side to 'Carry On' [1980 edit and remix]. Did not chart.

A song that fitted right into the Fleetwood Mac / Eagles / Billy Joel musical milieu of 1977. With its catchy, streamlined, jazzy piano and drums (Craig Doerge and Russ Kunkel), subtle slide guitar and bubbling percussion this can almost come off a Steely Dan album. The singing, in three-part harmony throughout, is gorgeous. Crosby said about it:

> Over and over again songs occur to me just as I'm dropping off to sleep, when the busy mind gets out of the way. I was 200 miles offshore and woke up in my bunk at 4 AM to transcribe these lyrics as if taking dictation. I learned to do that from a science fiction author friend of mine, a guy named William Gibson. I said, 'You know, does this happen to you? Do things come to you just as you're falling asleep when the sort of waking mind is going out?' And you know really heads have got a lot of levels and it seems as if another level gets, gets a shot at the steering wheel for a minute as you're on the way out, that, that makes longer leaps of connection. And, and somehow all of a sudden words are coming to you. A voice said to me, 'Shadow Captain of a charcoal grey ship / Trying to give the light the slip' ... It's about what many of my songs are about: Who is at the wheel? It's delving inside the cranial swamp, trying to figure out what matters, and why. It said a whole bunch of things I wanted to get said for a long time. I gave the lyrics to Craig Doerge and he wrote the music.

The result is a dynamic song that starts as a ballad, has a but kicks into gear and lifts away with a brilliant chorus – 'Who guides this ship / Dreaming through the seas? / Turning and searching / Whichever way you please.' 'The lyrics are some of Crosby's most interesting and poetic,' writes Alan Pattinson, 'with his unnamed shadow captain and his charcoal ship seemingly controlled by an outside force the navigator longs to see.'

'[This song's] conceit – travelling on a vessel guided by a hand whose purposes are incomprehensible – is spun out surely and poetically.' Peter Herbst, *Rolling Stone*, 17 June 1977

Go back and listen to 'Shadow Captain' – you might have forgotten just how good it is.

'See the Changes' (Stills)

A confident, stirring re-recording of a song first attempted during the 1973 CSNY sessions, hence 'Ten years singing right out loud': ten years since Stills started as a folkie in Greenwich Village. This version is wholly acoustic – just guitar and those glimmering voices. 'See the Changes' can be heard as a more mature, wiser answer not only to the difficulty in writing new songs but also in simply staying alive.

'It ain't easy rearranging / And it gets harder as you get older.' The production of the three-part harmony in the choruses is lovely, as good as anything from *Crosby, Stills & Nash*. A new remix is included on the 2013 box set *Carry On*.

'Carried Away' (Nash)

Released as the b-side of 'I Give You Give Blind', 1978.

'Carried Away' is delicate, perhaps a little too twee, even for Graham Nash. The melody is strong and the craft is palpable, especially the final harmony. But Nash has better songs here. One assumes he is checking adulterous impulses, but such analysis is often opaque. Certainly Nash is musing on what might have been. Jazz bassist Jimmy Haslip is criminally underused here.

As with the other three Nash-composed songs on this album, 'Carried Away' was written on piano. Despite his still-developing skills on the instrument, the switch in composition tool gives a different feel to these numbers compared to earlier guitar-based songs. 'Carried Away' and 'Cathedral' from this album, with the earlier 'Wind on the Water', 'Another Sleep Song' and others show a marked maturity in Nash's songwriting, Nash does not play guitar on *CSN* at all.

'Fair Game' (Stills)

Released as a single, 1977. B-side 'Anything at All'. Highest chart position: 43 (US).

A minor US hit in 1977, their first single to miss the top 40, this angular Stills song, which returns to his favourite Latin setting, has perhaps the worst two-line rhyme in musical history: 'The ones you never notice are the ones you have to watch / She's pleasant and she's friendly while she's looking at your crotch.'

The acoustic guitar solo is a killer, though. And for once drummer Joe Vitale adds to the vitality of the arrangement rather than simply trying to keep up.

'Anything at All' (Crosby)

Released as the b-side of 'Fair Game', 1977.

Some gentle self-reflection from David Crosby, who pokes fun at himself. Craig Doerge provides some luscious piano as Crosby's deeply-felt and starkly honest lyrics engender some superb singing. 'You see beneath the surface of the mud, there's more mud here. Surprise!'

The central section with the wordless rising vocal refrain and a fat 'hmmmmm' from Crosby is simply magnificent.

'Cathedral' (Nash)

One of Graham Nash's best songs surely? There are startling dynamics here, as an initially quiet and atmospheric song propels into fourth gear in the epic chorus. Stirring string arrangements underpin Crosby, Stills and Nash's perfect vocals. Always a highlight in live performances, this is a shining gem in the Nash back catalogue.

Graham Nash: 'Inspired by an acid trip taken at Winchester Cathedral on my thirty-second birthday [2 February 1974]. I lost who I was and where I was in that experience. It ended twenty hours later lying on my back in the middle of Stonehenge. In Nash's own words, spinning back to the early '70s:

> The incident was: getting up in the morning at 6:00, getting in this old Rolls-Royce that we'd hired for the day, going over to this dealer's in London and picking up some acid, dropping the acid and then going through Richmond Park with the ultimate goal of ending up in Stonehenge – and we went through Winchester on the way. The experience in Winchester Cathedral was probably my favourite acid trip I've taken. I was walking down the aisle, one of the aisles, there were graves on the floor and one of them attracted my attention and my legs started to waver, not shake, but just waver, you know, like a divining rod – it was real strange. I looked down and this guy had died on February 2nd 1799. I began to write a piece of music with no lyrics and that was the feeling of what it was I wanted to say. But trying to hone down the overwhelming series of feelings I had into some cohesive form, understandable to other people, was a long process.

A different mix, more dramatic and with a piano introduction, is on Nash's box set *Reflections*. The live version on the *No Nukes* album is better still.

'Dark Star' (Stills)

Released as the b-side to 'Just a Song before I Go', 1977.

Based on that bubbly opening guitar riff and stuffed full of percussion, this is perhaps the best of Stills' Latin-influenced songs. Mostly coloured by acoustic guitar and electric piano, this commercial song would become a beast in concert, electric and loud.

The exposed, honest and self-revealing lyrics are, according to Nash's memoirs, about Stills' relationship with Joan Baez. 'Love songs written for you, it's been going down for years / But to sing what's in my heart seems more honest than the tears.'

Stills has neither denied nor confirmed this.

'Just a Song Before I Go' (Nash)

Released as a single, 1977. B-side 'Dark Star'. Highest chart position: 7 (US).

Catchy and commercial, 'Just a Song Before I Go' was CSN's come-back hit, reaching #7 in the US, the band's highest-ever placement in the singles chart. 'Graham was at home in Hawaii about to go off on tour,' says David Crosby. 'The guy who was going to take him to the airport said, 'We've got fifteen minutes, I'll bet you can't write a song in that amount of time.' Well, you don't smart off to Nash like that, he'll do it. This is the result.'

It's pleasant enough and Stills adds some understated lead guitar. If songs like these get the meatier material before the public then it's done its job, right? 'This was our biggest hit single,' says Nash. 'Like Joe Walsh said, if I knew it was going to be such a big hit I would have written a better song.'

A demo version recorded at Rudy Records, San Francisco in November 1976 was released in 2018 on *Over the Years*.

'Run from Tears' (Stills)

A gruff, bluesy Stills song which revisits some of his past moods and chord changes. Halfway through side two of this album 'Run from Tears' provides a change of mood and sounds alternately relaxed and anxious. He was presumably reflecting on the breakdown of his marriage ('I am drowning / And I am fighting. / Something special / Is in me dying…'). Stills gets to cut loose on electric guitar for the first time on the album. Kudos here, too, to Michael Finnegan's swirling organ and Gerald Johnson's funky bass.

'Cold Rain' (Nash)

A grey, moody, sometimes poignant song about Manchester, written by Nash during the sessions after returning from his ailing mother's bedside in February 1977.

> It was so strange going back to Manchester this time. It was snowing and I

> went and stood on the very street corner where Allan Clarke and I had waited for the Everly Brothers years before [in 1960, outside the Midland Hotel]. And goddamn if everybody didn't look exactly the same. The exact same faces and ruddy complexions and the people scurrying by ... and they'll never change. But for a few good fortunes, I might still be there. No, I would not go back.

Despite this– maybe he'd forgotten that he'd said it, or hoped that we had – Nash performed the song at his first-ever solo hometown concert on 21 May 2016.

'In My Dreams' (Crosby)

Tucked away towards the end of the album, we have a minor masterpiece. David Crosby: 'I don't remember where I wrote it, but I remember recording it, and I love the guitar interplay between Stephen and me. We cut it together, two guitars and Russ Kunkel on drums.'

Those sinuous guitars play against each other perfectly: Crosby's guitar is in the left stereo channel, Stills' in the right. Vocals are split likewise, Crosby centre, Nash left and Stills right.

It's a typical multi-part Crosby song, shifting and changing, the latest in a long line of songs about the mind's unconscious or subconscious ruminations– see The Everly Brothers, Bobby Darin, Roy Orbison, Ella Fitzgerald, Supertramp, Fleetwood Mac and many others. The double-time coda, written by Nash but uncredited, adds some smooth vibraphone.

'I Give You Give Blind' (Stills)

Released as a single, 1978. B-side 'Carried Away'. Did not chart.

A dramatic, tough song with a hard-edged bite, 'I Give You Give Blind' provides a powerful end to an excellent album– stinging guitar, singing strings, pounding drums and Stills' underappreciated piano playing. A 1980 remix without the strings was included on the 'best of' album *Replay*. This is also on the 2013 *Carry On* box set.

> What's so instantly striking about Crosby, Stills and Nash's CSN, their second group album in eight years, is that it sounds so much like the debut LP even though its makers are so vastly changed. Since CS&N, and later Y, were always at the vanguard of the conspicuous counterculture (always ready to hoist their tie-dyed freak flag at a moment's notice), their current reflection and hesitancy are especially interesting. And, because the music is so eerily familiar, the album communicates a kind of time warp (imagine if we knew in 1969 what we know now) that's compelling and troubling. Those who have been put off in the past by Graham Nash's moralising, David Crosby's precious intellectualising and Stephen Stills' brash solipsism are going to be relieved to find all three musicians dramatically grown up – but not at all smug. Nearly all of the album's material is disconsolate – full of disillusionment and

identity confusion – but it's honest and surprisingly humble. Though CSN's wistfully unhappy tone leaves its music a mite depressing, the fusion of talents is an extremely happy one. Stills' Latin rock breaks up Nash and Crosby's contemplative music without obtruding, and his voice adds a masculinity lacking in the pair's post-CS&N work. Indeed, Stills prevents Crosby and Nash from being cloying, and they restrain his usual stridency. They are not imitating their original sound – all have been through too long an evolution, musically and personally, to be the cute, absurdly optimistic vocal group that arose with the Sixties' slow downshift. They spawned a generation of imitators and admirers and pretty much shaped the group approach to harmonies in the Seventies. In the end, though, as I think CSN proves, Crosby, Stills and Nash are not about a technique, but about the effect three people have on each other.
Peter Herbst, Rolling Stone, 17 June 1977

Songs from the 1977 sessions which were recorded (or at least attempted) and remain unreleased.

'Ain't It Always' (Stills)
Later attempted for Stills' unreleased 1979 album. It's probably the 1979 version that was eventually released on *Man Alive!*

'As I Come of Age' (Stills)
Recorded in 1970, mixed for release in 1973 (but held back) then included on *Stills* in 1975. It was re-recorded in 1977 and again in 1978 (or possibly re-purposed from the previous year). This wouldn't be last time this song was re-visited.

'Down Behind the Waves' (Nash)
Later attempted during CSN's aborted 1978 sessions, and for both *Earth & Sky* and *Daylight Again*. Is 'Down Behind the Waves' the same as 'Beneath the Waves' from Nash's solo album *This Path Tonight* (2016)?

'Jigsaw' (Crosby / Nash)
Later attempted for Crosby's unreleased 1980 album and recorded but not used for the Crosby-Nash album that eventually became CSN's *Live It Up*.

'Mirage' (Nash)
A Nash song that is listed as being recorded in Miami in January 1977. Nothing else is known about it.

'Paper Glider' (Crosby)
This was supposedly a very personal song about Crosby's deceased girlfriend Christine Hinton. Also attempted during the abandoned 1978 sessions.

'Rock and Roll Ain't Wrong' (Stills), **'I Told You So'** (Stills), **'Fortune Tellin' Lady'** (Stills)
Three Stills songs that are otherwise unknown.

'Watched It All Go Down' (Nash)
Later attempted for both *Earth & Sky* and *Songs for Survivors*.

'We Will Go On' (Stills), **'Beaucoup Yumbo'** (Stills)
Both later recorded for and released on *Thoroughfare Gap*.

In addition, 'Blackbird' was re-recorded. Stills also laid down a version of his venerable 'Treetop Flyer' which he has returned to many times since the mid-1970s. It was later recorded for and released on *Stills Alone*.

1982: Daylight Again

David Crosby: vocals; piano on 'Delta'
Stephen Stills: vocals; guitars all tracks except 'Delta', 'Song for Susan' and 'Might As Well Have A Good Time'; keyboards on 'Turn Your Back on Love' and 'Since I Met You'; banjo on 'Daylight Again'; percussion on 'Too Much Love to Hide'
Graham Nash: vocals; rhythm guitar on 'Turn Your Back on Love' and 'Into the Darkness'; harmonica on 'You Are Alive'; piano on 'Song for Susan'; organ on 'Into the Darkness'; percussion on 'Too Much Love to Hide'
and
Richard T. Bear: keyboards on 'Southern Cross'
Joel Bernstein: acoustic guitar on 'Wasted on the Way' and 'Song for Susan'
Craig Doerge: keyboards on 'Turn Your Back on Love', 'Wasted on the Way', 'Delta', 'Song for Susan' and 'Might as Well Have a Good Time'
Jay Ferguson: organ on 'Song for Susan'
Michael Finnigan: keyboards on 'Turn Your Back on Love', 'Southern Cross', 'Into the Darkness', 'Since I Met You', 'Too Much Love to Hide', 'You Are Alive' and 'Might As Well Have a Good Time'; backing vocals on 'Turn Your Back on Love', 'Southern Cross', 'Since I Met You' and 'You Are Alive'
Art Garfunkel: vocals on 'Southern Cross' and 'Daylight Again'
Bob Glaub: bass on 'Wasted on the Way'
Wayne Goodwin: fiddle on 'Wasted on the Way'
Russ Kunkel: drums on 'Wasted on the Way,' 'Delta,' and 'Song for Susan'
Joe Lala: percussion on 'Wasted on the Way', 'Southern Cross', 'Into the Darkness', 'Since I Met You', 'Too Much Love to Hide' and 'You Are Alive'
Dean Parks: electric guitar on 'Delta'
George 'Chocolate' Perry: bass all tracks except 'Wasted on the Way', 'Delta', 'Song for Susan', 'Might as Well Have a Good Time' and 'Daylight Again'
Jeff Porcaro: drums on 'Since I Met You'
Timothy B. Schmit: vocals on 'Turn Your Back on Love', 'Wasted on the Way', 'Southern Cross', 'Song for Susan' and 'You Are Alive', bass on 'Song for Susan'
Leland Sklar: bass on 'Delta'
Michael Stergis: guitars all tracks except 'Delta', 'Might as Well Have a Good Time' and 'Daylight Again'
Gerry Tolman: guitar on 'Too Much Love to Hide'
Joe Vitale: drums on 'Turn Your Back on Love', 'Southern Cross', 'Into the Darkness', 'Too Much Love to Hide' and 'You Are Alive'
Roberleigh Barnhart, Miguel Martinez, Ernie Ehrhardt – cellos on 'Song for Susan'
Recorded 1980-1981 at Rudy Records, Devonshire Sound and Sea West. Produced by David Crosby, Stephen Stills and Graham Nash.
Released: 21 June 1982 (US). Highest chart position: 8 (US), did not chart in the UK.

Daylight Again **was never intended to be a Crosby, Stills and Nash album at all. After CSN's tour of July-August 1978 each of the three started work on new solo albums. Nash's *Earth & Sky* was recorded between November 1978 and**

October 1979 and released in February 1980. Crosby started work a new solo album in late 1979. He took 'Drive My Car' from the April 1978 CSN sessions, 'Distances' which was started in during those CSN sessions and finished in subsequent Crosby & Nash sessions, and recorded several more new songs. The album was completed in mid-1980.

Stills' album, produced by Barry Beckett and to have been called *Southern Cross* was rejected by Atlantic. It was re-purposed as a Stills/Nash project. The title track and 'You Are Alive' were taken forward to new versions later that year. Sessions for this project commenced in October 1980 at Nash's Rudy Records in Los Angeles with Stills' regular backup band. Recording continued with vocal overdubs in Hawaii the following Spring. In Crosby's absence, the third voice was provided by Timothy B Schmit of The Eagles, Art Garfunkel and session player Michael Finnegan.

The sessions went smoothly, resulting in far more tracks than were needed for the album. Other songs reportedly recorded include: 'Alibis' (Nash), 'Cadillac' (unknown) 'Dangerous Woman on the Loose' (Stills), 'Down Behind The Waves' (Nash), 'Down On The Tubes' (Nash), 'Every Grain of Sand' (the Bob Dylan song), 'Here On The Same Boat' (unknown), 'Into Valhalla' (Nash), 'Lonely Side Of Me' (Nash), 'Look at my Face' (unknown), 'Maria Pia' (unknown), 'On the Other Side of Town' (Nash, recorded by Crosby and Nash in 2004), 'One Way Ride' (Stills), 'Sailor' (Nash), 'The Award' (unknown), 'Tomorrow Is Another Day' (Stills) and 'You Might Be Loved' (Stills).

Stills and Nash presented an album to their record company in August 1981. 'From the start,' Nash says, 'Atlantic was not fantastically interested in a Stills-Nash album, because it was an unknown quantity. They wanted a CSN album.'

Stills and Nash initially resisted as they had paid for $400,000 worth of sessions themselves. In 1983, Nash would retcon this series of events by saying 'When I started listening to the work that Stephen and I had done, I swear I could hear Crosby's voice in there. It was like his voice was singing on the tracks. Very weird. Then I realised that he really wasn't there and I started to miss him.'

Nash called Crosby in mid-November 1981. Crosby's vocals were added to six Stills/Nash songs the following month, starting with 'Song for Susan'. Stills' and Nash's vocals were overdubbed onto three songs from Crosby's rejected solo album in January and March 1982: 'Delta', 'Melody' and 'Might as Well Have a Good Time'. One further track was recorded between January and March 1982: Stills' 'Since I Met You'.

Despite its long gestation, *Daylight Again* is a good, if inconsistent, album, with some excellent songs: especially, and perhaps ironically, Crosby's 'Delta', one of his best ever.

'This was, by far, one of the most frustrating projects of my life,' Nash reflected. 'Sometimes, it was hard to see the whole and get a sense of CSN as a unit. But we pulled it together. I'm very proud of this record. It took far too long to complete, but it was worth it.'

'Turn Your Back on Love' (Stills / Nash / Stergis)

'Turn Your Back on Love' is a laid-back, moody rock song based on a guitar riff by Graham Nash. Stills took Nash's chord changes and, working with guitarist Michael Stergis, came back with a completed song. It features a tremendous lead vocal by Stills, with Mike Finnegan taking Crosby's vocal part. The song is driven by Chocolate Perry's pumping bass guitar– in concert, the songs would become a monster with three electric guitars pushing that riff.

There is an unreleased alternative take available on bootleg, with mostly different verse lyrics and none at all in the chorus. Even in this unfinished state, it sounds like a classic.

'Wasted on the Way' (Nash)

Released as a single, 1982. B-side 'Delta'. Highest chart position: 9 (US).

> We have wasted an enormous amount of time on petty issues that should never have kept us from making music.
> Graham Nash

This is a smooth, laid back country-pop song with a universal theme: it's not too late to make up for time lost and opportunities missed. The second verse is terrific – 'When you were young, did you question all the answers? / Did you envy all the dancers who had all the nerve? / Look round you know. You must go for what you wanted. / Look at all my friends who did and got what they deserved.'

Life is too short to fake it.

Like many of CSN's best songs, it's sung in three-part harmony – it's the Eagles' Timothy B Schmit taking the middle harmony in place of Crosby. His lighter tenor voice is so close to Nash's that its sounds double-tracked. A demo version by Stills, Nash and Schmidt recorded at Sea-West, Oahu, in October 1980 was released in 2018 on *Over the Years*. The live version on *Allies* – three voices, two guitars – is quite lovely. Don't watch it on YouTube or the DVD though as Crosby is on another planet entirely. When Nash reunited with The Hollies in 1983, they too performed 'Wasted on the Way' in concert.

'Southern Cross' (Stills / Curtis / Curtis)

Released as a single, 1982. B-side 'Into the Darkness'. Highest chart position: 18 (US).

An effortlessly commercial song, skilfully adapted from another song altogether, hence the joint writing credit to Rick and Michael Curtis.

'The Curtis Brothers brought me a wonderful song called 'Seven League Boots' [recorded in 1975],' recalls Stephen Stills. 'But it drifted around too much. I re-wrote a new set of words and added a different chorus, a story about a long boat trip I took after my divorce. It's about using the power of the universe to heal your wounds.'

A song about picking yourself up after a fall, 'Southern Cross' is Stills' sailing song, a worthy addition to Crosby's 'The Lee Shore' and 'Shadow Captain' and forthcoming 'Compass' and 'Radio'. The chorus is uplifting, despite its slight air of loss: 'I have been around the world looking for that woman girl / Who knows love can endure / And you know it will.'

Surprisingly, 'Southern Cross' is CSN's most-performed song: over 800 times since 1983. Jimmy Buffett has included the song in his own setlists for twenty years or more.

'Into the Darkness' (Nash)

Released as the b-side of 'Southern Cross', 1982.

'Into the Darkness' wasn't supposed to be on *Daylight Again* at all. Its title certainly sits uneasily alongside the name of its parent album. But with 'Feel Your Love' being pulled at the last minute as being too similar to the Rose Royce song 'Love Don't Live Here Anymore', Stills and Nash retrieved 'Into the Darkness' from their 1980 duo sessions. It can be heard as a straight response to 'Out of the Darkness' from *Whistling Down the Wire,* addressing David Crosby directly. 'Into the darkness soon you'll be sinking,' Nash sings. 'What are you doing? What can you be thinking?'

If this is uncomfortable to listen to as a fan, Crosby himself was understandably pissed that such a negative song went on the album, especially when his own songs were overlooked. 'That song didn't need to be put on there. I could tell it's about me and I don't like it. They could have put one of my songs on there, like 'Melody' Why did that have to get left off?'

He has a point.

'Delta' (Crosby)

Released as the b-side of 'Wasted on the Way', 1982.

A key song in Crosby's back catalogue: as he says sings in the lyrics, 'Delta' is a song about 'choice' and 'chance'. David Crosby:

> I wrote that stoned half-way out of my mind on my boat. It was the last complete song I'd written until I kicked drugs in prison several years later and my songwriting came back to me. I had pieces of the tune in my head and one day I ran into Jackson Browne in Santa Barbara. He took me over to Warren Zevon's place and got me to sit down at the piano and work at the song. I wanted to smoke the pipe, I kept saying, 'Just gimme a minute, just gimme a minute,' but Jackson kept insisting I stay at the piano and finish the song.

Most of the vocals on the released version are Crosby alone. 'My harmony stacks were so tight,' he said, 'we left most of them in. Graham and Stephen barely sing on that song.'

'Crosby and Nash sing the last verse alone, in pristine harmony,' writes Alan Pattinson. 'Their movement away from each other on the key change 'in my sleep' is simply one of the most moving things I have ever heard.'

The beautiful bass line is played by Leland Sklar, veteran of thousands of sessions, and a member of the 1970s instrumental band The Section who performed studio and in-concert backup for James Taylor, Jackson Brown, Crosby & Nash and many others.

The live version on the *Daylight Again* DVD is heart-breaking. Crosby, accompanying himself on piano, is utterly out of it and yet is able to sing like an angel. And, against the odds, he's still here 40 years later, still singing 'Delta' at nearly 80 years of age.

'Since I Met You' (Stills / Stergis)

The only new song recorded after Crosby joined the project. It's a by-the-numbers Stills rocker, co-written with live band member Michael Stergis. Toto's drummer Jeff Porcaro sits in. 'Since I Met You' can't possibly revisit the heights of side one of *Daylight Again* and, despite a lively guitar solo, sounds like an outtake from a late period Stills solo album.

'Too Much Love to Hide' (Stills / Tolman)

Released as a single, 1983. B-side 'Song for Susan'. Highest chart position: 69 (US).

A twin to 'Since I Met You'. It was co-written with CSN's manager Gerry Tolman who also plays guitar on this recording. Even though this forgettable song was a minor hit single in 1983 it surely should have been replaced in this album's running order by one of Crosby's songs?

'Song for Susan' (Nash)

Release as the b-side of 'Too Much Love to Hide', 1983.

A syrupy ballad for Nash's wife which might have sat better on a solo album. Crosby's harmony vocals in the chorus make the song– he might have been singing for himself on the lines 'Fooling myself about how to exist / All by myself there was much I had missed / You came and showed me what happiness is.' The cellos are understated and effective.

'You Are Alive' (Stills / Stergis)

Another weak song, a sluggish ballad from Stills' rejected solo album, glossy and contemporary-sounding but listless.

'Might as Well Have a Good Time' (Henske / Doerge)

'Might as Well Have a Good Time' was written by long-time collaborator Craig Doerge and his wife, singer Judy Henske. Some might argue that the already-recorded songs 'Drive My Car', 'Melody' or 'Distances' might have been better choices, but the sentiment and the craft on 'Might as Well Have a Good Time' are palpable. Crosby sings it beautifully. Stills' and Nash's harmonies were added later: the original arrangement was included on the 2006 re-issue of *Daylight Again*.

'It was how I felt,' Crosby told Dave Zimmer. 'Even if things aren't like you want them to be, you might as well have a good time.'

That could have been Crosby's memorial.

'Daylight Again / Find the Cost of Freedom' (Stills)

A wry highlight of the album and of Stills' career. The song had been floating about for several years, born out of Stills' riffing the chords to 'Find the Cost of Freedom' and developing lyrics off the cuff.

> I was out on tour and we'd done four nights running. I was in Williamsburg, Virginia, and burnt out and dead tired. At the end of the concert I began to play the song. I didn't have any words, but I continued to play. I closed my eyes and went into a trance and saw a movie. It was a talking dream where I went back 112 years, to the Civil War. The lyrics just flowed through me like an automatic poem. I sang them as they came into my head and a whole story unfolded. When the concert was over I rushed backstage and madly tried to reconstruct the lyrics.

Stills' performance of this song with Manassas at Winterland in October 1973 is simply astonishing. The 1982 version edits those freeform lyrics to six brilliant lines:

> Daylight again, following me to bed / I think about a hundred years ago, how my fathers bled / I think I see a valley, covered with bones in blue / All the brave soldiers that cannot get older been askin' after you / Hear the past a callin', from Armegeddon's side / If everyone's talkin' and no-one is listening, how can we decide?

The link to the song's genesis is made explicit as this segues into a line from 'Find the Cost of Freedom' sung by Stills, Nash and Art Garfunkel. When Crosby joined the sessions they tried to re-record as CSN but Garfunkel's vocal was so good that they kept the original. This sounds quite different to the 1970 version. Even though it's in the same D major key, both Nash and Garfunkel sing above Still's melody line, whereas previously Nash was above and Crosby below.

Bonus tracks on 2006 reissue

'Raise a Voice' (Nash / Stills)

Take from *Allies*.

'Feel Your Love' (Stills / Nash)

The chorus' similarity to the Rose Royce song 'Love Don't Live Here Anymore' precluded this excellent song's inclusion on *Daylight Again*. 'It was one of those cases where something you heard in the middle of a busy day takes up residence in your subconscious and just floats to the surface,' Stills said. 'Garfunkel brought it up. I was just floored.'

Stills tried to agree on a publishing deal with the song's writer Miles Gregory but nothing could be settled; Nash's *Into the Darkness* was added to the album instead. The song was also considered for *American Dream* and after years of floating around as a ropey bootleg was finally added to the CD re-issue of *Daylight Again*.

'Tomorrow Is Another Day' (Stills)

This is a Stills rocker with lots of his trademark wah-wah guitar. Crosby is very noticeable in the vocal mix.

'Might as Well Have a Good Time' (Henske / Doerge)

The version intended for Crosby's solo album– it's the same as the one on *Daylight Again* but without Stills and Nash.

Other contemporary songs

'As I Come of Age' (Stills)

Another attempt at a CSN version of a track recorded many times over the years. Recorded at Rudy Records, Los Angeles, in January 1981. This was scheduled for the unreleased *As I Come of Age* album in 1985. Released on the *CSN* box set in 1991.

'Dear Mr. Fantasy' (Winwood / Capaldi / Wood)

From the Stills and Nash sessions in Los Angeles, 17 November 1980, but dropped from the final running order for *Daylight Again*. It was also pegged for release on the unreleased CSN album *As I Come of Age* in 1985. This can be heard on the *CSN* box set. An alternative 14-minute take circulates amongst collectors. Stephen Stills:

> Stevie Winwood was always my favourite singer, that blue-eyed sound. It had been our ambition from the start to convince him to join Crosby, Stills and Nash – I wanted an organ player who could sing the blues. He was exceptionally kind to me, but every time I trudged across the moors to see him, he was always occupied. We've recorded 'Dear Mr. Fantasy' a number of times, beginning in 1970. It was intended as an homage. Hats off, Stevie.

'Melody' (Crosby)

A track from Crosby's unreleased 1980 solo album with vocals added by Stills and Nash in January 1982. Amazingly, this was not used on *Daylight Again*. The basic recording was overdubbed in 1986 and 1988 and, with Stills and Nash's vocals removed, was released on Crosby's *Oh Yes I Can*.

1983: Allies

Personnel:
David Crosby: vocals, guitars
Stephen Stills: vocals, guitars, keyboards
Graham Nash: vocals, guitars, keyboards
and
on 1977 recordings:
Craig Doerge: keyboards
Joe Lala: percussion
George 'Chocolate' Perry: bass;
Joe Vitale: drums
on 1982 recordings:
Mike Finnigan: keyboards, vocals
James Newton Howard: keyboards
George 'Chocolate' Perry: bass
Michael Stergis: electric guitar
Joe Vitale: drums
On 1983 recordings:
Craig Doerge: keyboards
James Newton Howard: keyboards
Danny Kortchmar: electric guitar
George 'Chocolate' Perry: bass
Jeff Porcaro: drums
Michael Stergis: electric guitar
Efrain Toro: percussion
Recorded at The Summit, Houston, 22 November 1977; New Universal Amphitheatre, Universal City, 27 November 1982; Portland Memorial Coliseum, 5 December 1982. Studio tracks at Devonshire Studios, Los Angeles, March-April 1983. Produced by Steven Stills, Graham Nash and Stanley Johnson.
Released: 6 June 1983 (US). Highest chart position: 43 (US), did not chart in the UK.

The first CSN live album. Well, mostly. The opening two songs are new 1983 studio recordings: 'War Games' and 'Raise a Voice'.

The rest of the album, mostly recorded at the New Universal Amphitheatre in Universal City, CA, is robust and enjoyable but hardly essential. It comprises tight and agreeable live versions of 'Dark Star' from *CSN*, 'Turn Your Back on Love' and 'Wasted on the Way' from *Daylight Again*, 'Barrel of Pain' from Nash's most recent solo album and crowd-pleasing dips into the long-gone '60s with Lennon / McCartney's 'Blackbird' and Stills' 'For What It's Worth'. David Crosby is clearly in poor health. Indeed, the versions of 'Shadow Captain' and a cover of Joni's 'He Played Real Good for Free' included here were recorded on CSN's 1977 tour, when Crosby was in better voice.

The DVD, *Daylight Again*, despite showing Crosby utterly fried, has some great performances, especially 'Delta' and 'Treetop Flyer'. Some of the tracks on the DVD were released on a freebie CD given away with the Daily Mail in the UK in 2005: 'Love the One You're With', 'Wooden Ships', 'Long Time Gone', 'Teach Your Children', 'Suite: Judy Blue Eyes', 'For What It's Worth' and 'Wasted on the Way'. The entire DVD soundtrack has been unofficially released in Japan as the CD *Live in LA*.

'War Games' (Stills)

Released a single (b/w 'Shadow Captain') in June 1983. Highest chart position: 45 (US).

A fast-paced Stills song with a driving keyboard riff, written for the soundtrack of the 1983 sci-fi thriller of the same name. It was directed by John Badham and featuring a young Matthew Broderick.

'War Games' was recorded at Devonshire Studios, Los Angeles, March-April 1983 with a top-notch band: Craig Doerge, James Newton Howard (composer of choice for the director M. Night Shyamalan and later an 8-time Oscar nominee for his film soundtrack work), Danny Kortchmar, Michael Stergis, George 'Chocolate' Perry, Jeff Porcaro and Efrain Toro.

The film's producers didn't use the song, but CSN released it anyway both as a single and as the opening track on *Allies*. Stills and Nash performed a tough, rocking live version at Muddy Waters Café in September 1983, broadcast on NBC's *Rock and Roll Tonite*.

'Raise a Voice' (Nash / Stills)

Released a single (b / w 'For What It's Worth') in 1983. Did not chart.

'Raise a Voice' was recorded at Devonshire Studios, Los Angeles in March-April 1983. It's a rare fifty-fifty Nash and Stills collaboration. Stills took Nash's waltz-time chords changes and switched them to common 4/4. The lyrics revisit Stills' first solo album: 'Do we run? Do we stop? / Do we lie down? I think not. / There's an answer that we've got. / We are not helpless.'

Crosby's vocals were added after the fact. You can barely hear him. 'Raise a Voice' appears on both Nash's and Stills' box sets – *Reflections* (remixed, boosting Nash's vocals) and *Carry On*.

'Turn Your Back on Love' (Stills / Nash / Stergis)

A powerful, guitar-heavy, very funky version with a great, strong Stills vocal. It has a much fuller sound than the studio take from *Daylight Again*.

'Barrel of Pain' (Nash)

A slow-burning version of the key song from Nash's 1980 solo album *Earth & Sky*. It has amazing bass playing from Chocolate Perry and a dynamic closing section featuring powerhouse vocals by keyboardist Michael Finnegan.

'Shadow Captain' (Crosby / Doerge)
Recorded in 1977, this is a faithful and excellent live interpretation of the opening track from *CSN*. Craig Doerge is on great form here.

'Dark Star' (Stills)
Once again, Chocolate Perry's brilliant bass-playing underpins a tight, loud version of a key Stills track from *CSN*, with twin electric guitars, washes of organ and skittering percussion.

'Blackbird' (Lennon / McCartney)
The first release of a song that CSN had been performing for years. CSN's acoustic performances, when they are 'on', are unassailable. This is quite lovely.

'He Played Real Good for Free' (Mitchell)
Crosby sings a Joni Mitchell song first released on *Ladies of the Canyon* in April 1970. Gorgeous.

'Wasted on the Way' (Nash)
A fully acoustic version, less energetic than the studio take but improved without the fiddle.

'For What It's Worth' (Stills)
A slightly arthritic but crowd-pleasing take on the Buffalo Springfield song.

1988: American Dream

Personnel:
David Crosby: vocals; acoustic guitar on 'Clear Blue Skies' and 'Compass'
Stephen Stills: vocals; guitars on 'Name of Love', 'Don't Say Goodbye', 'Nighttime for the Generals', 'Drivin' Thunder', 'Clear Blue Skies', 'That Girl', 'Soldiers of Peace' and 'Night Song'; keyboards on 'American Dream' and 'Got It Made';bass synthesizer on 'Don't Say Goodbye'; bass, synthesizer and handclaps on 'Night Song'; percussion on 'Drivin' Thunder'
Graham Nash: vocals; piano on 'Don't Say Goodbye'; electric guitar on 'Nighttime for the Generals'; keyboards and harmonica on 'Clear Blue Skies'
Neil Young: vocals; guitars on all tracks except 'Compass'; all instruments on 'This Old House'; piano on 'Don't Say Goodbye'; harmonica on 'Compass'; percussion on 'Name of Love' and 'Feel Your Love'
and
Chad Cromwell: drums on 'That Girl'
Mike Finnegan: organ on 'Nighttime for the Generals'; keyboards, backing vocals on 'Soldiers of Peace'
Bob Glaub: bass on 'American Dream', 'Got It Made', 'Name of Love', 'Nighttime for the Generals', 'Drivin' Thunder', 'Clear Blue Skies', 'That Girl' and 'Soldiers of Peace'
Joe Lala: percussion on 'Got It Made', 'Shadowland', 'Clear Blue Skies' and 'That Girl'; drums on 'Soldiers of Peace'
Joe Vitale: drums on 'American Dream', 'Got It Made', 'Name of Love', 'Don't Say Goodbye', 'Nighttime for the Generals', 'Drivin' Thunder', 'Clear Blue Skies' and 'Night Song'; vocals and all instruments on 'Shadowland'; keyboards on 'Clear Blue Skies', 'That Girl', 'Compass' and 'Soldiers of Peace'; synthesizer on 'Don't Say Goodbye'; percussion on 'Drivin' Thunder' and 'Feel Your Love'; vibraphone on 'Feel Your Love'
and The Bluenotes: Tommy Bray, Claude Callilet, Larry Cragg, John Fumo, Steve Lawrence – horns on 'That Girl'
Recorded April 1987 – September1988 at Redwood Digital, Woodside, California. April 1987: 'Shadowland'; February 1988: 'Name of Love'. March 1988: 'American Dream', 'Got It Made', 'Nighttime for the Generals', 'Drivin' Thunder', 'Clear Blues Skies', 'Compass'. May 1988: 'This Old House', 'That Girl'. July 1988: 'Feel Your Love', 'Night Song'. September 1988: 'Don't Say Goodbye', 'Soldiers of Peace'.
Released 1 November 1988 (US). Highest chart positions 16 (US), 55 (UK)

It's almost impossible to describe the levels of anticipation and the crushing disappointment when this album was released in late 1988.

As with other rock acts who rose to fame in the '60s and early '70s, the sterile late-'80s production practically suffocates *American Dream*. So many of the 'veteran' artists have one of these '80s albums lurking in their catalogues somewhere. They are almost always terrible. Think of *Dog Eat Dog* (Joni Mitchell, 1986), *Landing on Water* (Neil Young, 1986), *Press to Play* (Paul

McCartney, 1986), *Hold Your Fire* (Rush, 1987), *A Momentary Lapse of Reason* (Pink Floyd, 1987), *Never Let Me Down* (David Bowie, 1987). And yet there are two stone-cold classics hidden on side two of *American Dream*: 'Compass' and 'Feel Your Love'.

American Dream started as a CSN project with initial sessions in March-April 1987. Only 'Shadowland' survived to the finished CSNY album, although several songs were recorded including Crosby's 'He's an American', Stills' 'Lover' and Nash's 'Water from the Moon'.

Later that year, Neil Young followed up on a promise he'd made to David Crosby some years earlier: that he'd take part in another CSNY album if Crosby quit drugs.

'Everybody's concerned about David,' he told a Rockline caller in November 1983. 'He's a unique person and has a lot of problems that are unique to him. He's having a rough time. He really took a bad turn. I hope he gets himself together. I've told him that if he does get himself together and straightens himself up that I'll join the group again and we'll do something together. And that's all I can do, you know?'

He'd perhaps forgotten the lyrics of the song 'Thrasher' from his 1979 album *Rust Never Sleeps*. 'So I got bored and left them there / They were just deadweight to me / Better down the road without that load'.

> Yeah. Parts of ['Thrasher'] were [about CSN]. Just dead weight. Well, at that point, I felt like it was kind of dead weight for me. Not for them. For me. I could go somewhere and they couldn't go there. I wasn't going to pull them along; they were doing fine without me. It might have come off a little more harsh than I meant it, but once I write it I can't say, 'Oh, I'm going to hurt somebody's feelings.' Poetically and on feeling it made good sense to me and it came right out. I think I'd be doing it a disservice to change it based on what I think a reaction would be. I try not to do that.

The bulk of *American Dream* was recorded at Young's ranch, immediately after he completed work on *This Note's for You* (November 1987-January 1988). Sessions were contemporaneous with those for David Crosby's second album *Oh Yes I Can*, which was recorded mostly in April and May 1988. The album sold over one million copies and was a top twenty hit in the US.

> Forget the careerist compromise, dazed ennui, and soggy despair, and take this hustle for what it pretends to be and at some level is: four diehard hippies expressing themselves. Poor old guys can't leave politics alone--there's more ecology and militarism here than when they were figureheads of pop revolution, and though the rhetoric is predictable, the impulse has a woozy nobility. Not that that's ever been reason to pay Graham's ditties any mind, or that Stephen's steady-state egotism is redeemed by stray references to judges and changing the world. But while David's cocaine confessional makes 'Almost

Cut My Hair' seem self-abnegating, his 'Nighttime for the Generals' sure beats Sting. And Neil lends musical muscle and gets commercial muscle back. So, not as horrible as you expected--nor good enough to give a third thought.
Robert Christgau, *Village Voice*, 1988

A remix of *American Dream* with all that '80s gloss scraped away would reveal a collection of half-decent songs, struggling to breathe.

'American Dream' (Young)

Released as a single, 1988. B-side 'Compass'. Highest chart positions: 4 (US Mainstream Rock), 55 (UK).

Synthesised pipes, handclaps and bubbling bass open CNSY's second studio album. The song is a typical Neil Young dig on two aspects of modern life in 1987: the Iran-Contra scandal (the US sale of arms to Iran) and the downfall of Presidential candidate Gary Hart. The tone is not so far from the contemporary 'This Note's for You'. The recorded take is loaded with reverb.

'Don't know when things went wrong, it might have been when you were young and strong.' The song was first performed by Young in a solo acoustic arrangement on his 1987 tour. Crosby, Stills and Nash and Young performed a similar stripped-down version at the annual Bridge School concert in April 1988. It's a wholly different (and hugely enjoyable) song in its acoustic guise.

'American Dream' provided CSN(Y) with their second and final entry on the UK singles chart. The video is hilarious – check it out on YouTube.

'Got It Made' (Stills / Young)

Released as a single, 1989. Highest chart positions: 69 (US).

Electric piano and drums played in the bathroom down the hall colour this minor Stills song – this is the writer of 'Suite: Judy Blue Eyes' and '4 + 20'. 'This was written during the *American Dream* sessions with some help from Neil,' he said later '... but I was never satisfied with the way the song turned out.' The middle eight, Young's contribution, sounds flown in from another universe. Some fat Bluenotes-era lead guitar gives a few seconds of interest in this utterly forgettable and seemingly interminably long tune. Alarmingly, this is CSN(Y)'s only no. 1 single, going all the way on the US Mainstream Rock charts in 1989, based on radio play.

A far superior live version from CSN's United Nations concert on 18 November 1989 is included in the *CSN* box set. Stills plays piano in the best *4 Way Street* manner.

'Name of Love' (Young)

The reverb-laden drums and percussion hide what sounds at first like a half-decent Neil Young: slow down the tempo, strip the production gloss, write

Above: Stills, Crosby and Nash in 1969 - 'They are one person / They are two alone / They are three together / They are for each other.' (*Alamy*)

Below: Stills, Young, Crosby and Nash in 1973 – 'We lost it on the highway / Down the dotted line / You were going your way / I was going mine.' *(Atlantic)*

Left: Whereas vocally, *Crosby, Stills & Nash* is a product of their three voices blending together, musically, it belongs almost entirely to Stephen Stills. (*Atlantic*)

Right: *Déjà vu*. Neil Young's addition cast a long shadow over CSN. It was a career-defining, and possibly harmful, decision that has, ever since, resulted in unfair and often damning comparison between Young's work and CSN's. (*Atlantic*)

Right: *4 Way Street* is a faithful representation of a typical CSNY show, from the highs of the acoustic set to the lows of the protracted rock and roll jamming. (*Atlantic*)

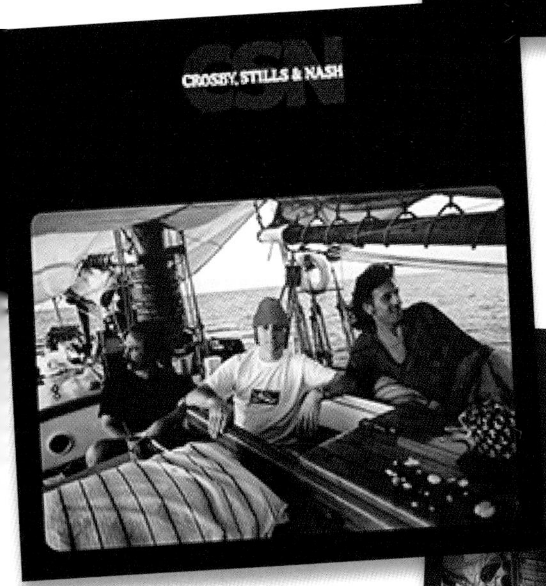

Left and below: The variant covers to 1977's *CSN*. The songs are strong, the performances spirited, the production uncluttered and slick. *CSN* is the trio's best-selling album. (*Atlantic*)

Nash and Crosby, harmonising — best friends for almost fifty years. 'I don't like David Crosby right now,' Nash said in 2016. 'He's been awful for me the last two years, just fucking awful. I've been there and saved his fucking ass for 45 years, and he treated me like shit. You can't do that to me.'

Right: Nash, Crosby, Young and Stills in 1970. When they were 'on', they were peerless. Those occasions were infrequent, but they have spent lifetimes trying to replicate them.

Left: Crosby, Stills, Nash, Young… and Jones. CSNYJ on *This is Tom Jones* in 1969.

Right: Crosby, Nash, Reeves and Young in 1969

Left: Graham Nash performs for the BBC in 1970. His tender songwriting and high tenor hide a steely determination.

Right: Nash and Crosby at the beginning of their successful duo career. Crosby looks 'very happy'.

Left: *Daylight Again* was never intended to be a Crosby, Stills and Nash album at all. Despite this, it is a good, if inconsistent, album with some excellent songs: especially, and perhaps ironically, Crosby's 'Delta', one of his best. (*Atlantic*)

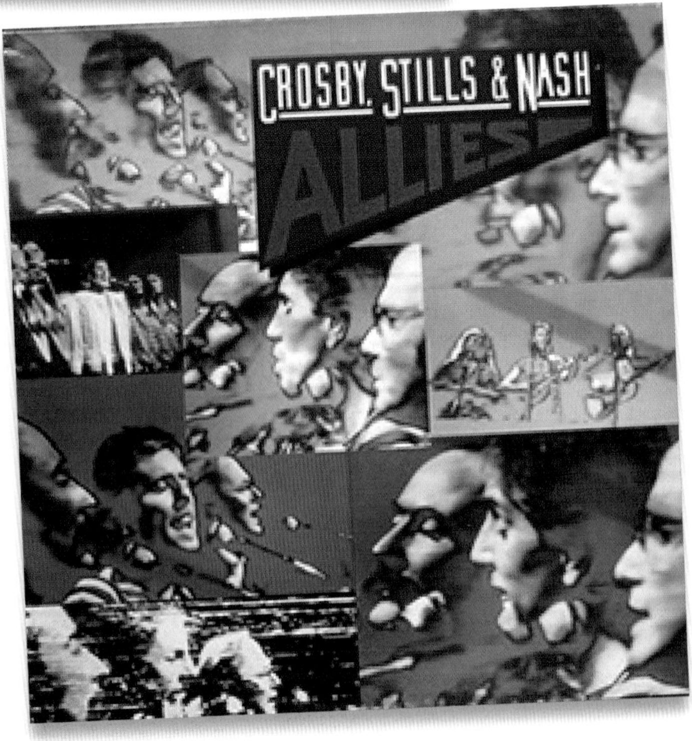

Right: 1983's *Allies*. Some decent live tracks and two new studio cuts. This album has been out of print for years, but is available to stream and download. (*Atlantic*)

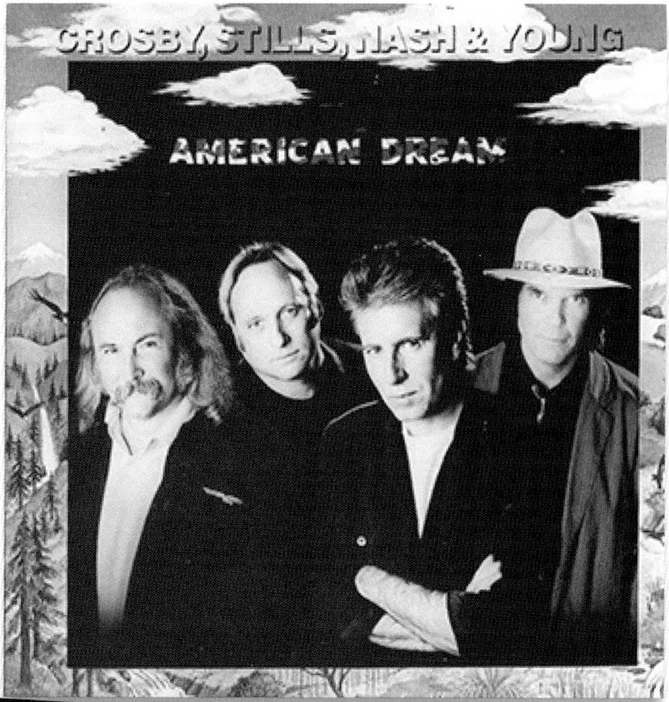

Right: It's almost impossible to describe the levels of anticipation and the crushing disappointment when *American Dream*, the first CSNY album for eighteen years, was released in late 1988. (*Atlantic*)

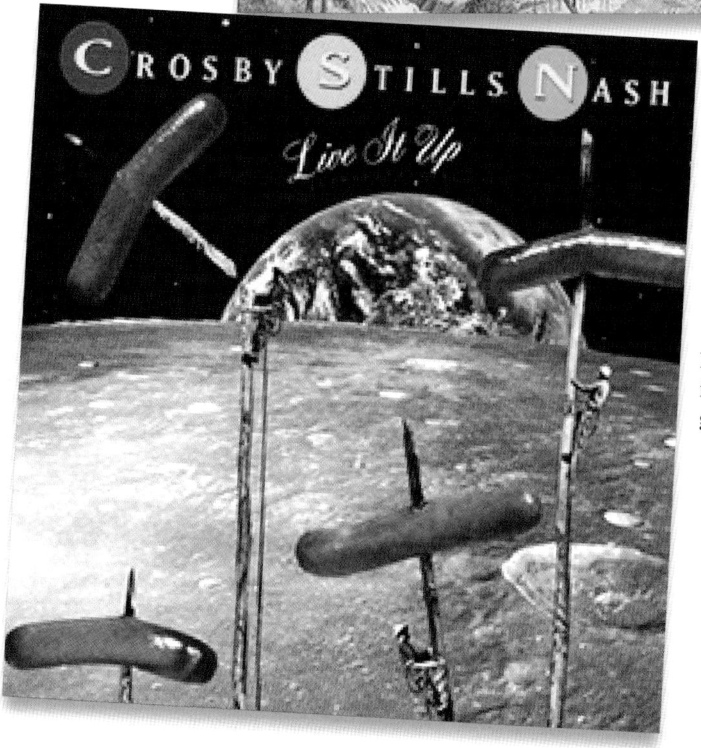

Left: *Live It Up* from 1990. It's not great. *(Atlantic*)

Left: Stills, Nash and Crosby sing 'Teach Your Children' at Live Aid in July 1985.

Right: David Crosby at Live Aid. He would soon spend nine months in a Texas state prison.

Left: Stills, Nash and Crosby at Live Aid. They would also reunite with Neil Young later in the afternoon.

Right: Stephen Stills in 1991 during *The Acoustic Concert* – his output from 1967 to 1973 is without peer.

Left and below: CSN doing what they do best – three voices and three guitars, at *The Acoustic Concert*.

Left: *After the Storm* (1994) – three-quarters of a great album. (*Atlantic*)

Right: *Looking Forward*, CSNY's third and last studio album does not reach the heights of *Déjà Vu*. Thankfully, neither does it trawl the depths of *American Dream*, but it's a close call. (*Reprise*)

Right: *Déjà Vu Live*. The last new CSNY album—a potpourri of live tracks from the 2008 tour. It is interesting, but hardly essential. (*Atlantic*)

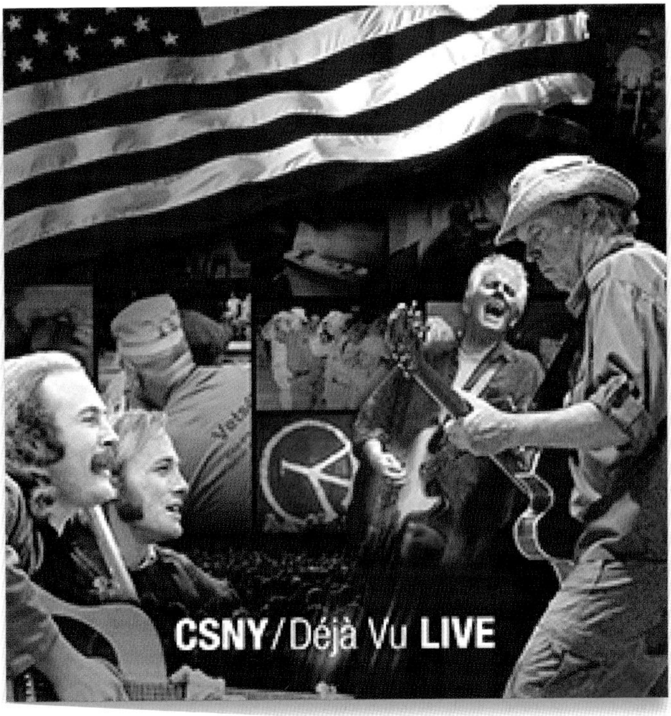

Left: *So Far* was a compilation album released mid-way through CSNY's US tour in Summer 1974. A 'best of' after just two albums? Record label cash-in ahoy! Graham Nash: 'We were totally against *So Far* coming out.' (*Atlantic*)

Above: Nash, Stills and Young discuss set-lists and running orders in 2008.

Above: Stephen Stills and Neil Young – 50 years as buddies and still playing together.

Above: CSNY on their last tour together in 2008.

Above: The Freedom of Speech tour, 2008. With Neil Young very much the dominant force, CSNY would perform most of Young's uncompromising *Living with War* album.

Left: CSN's acoustic concert DVD from 1991. The cover uses a group shot from 1977. (*Warner*)

Below: The *Greatest Hits* album from 2005. (*Rhino*)

Left: The CSN *Demos* album from 2009. (*Rhino*)

Right: *2012*. The most recent and presumably last new album from Crosby, Stills and Nash, recorded during the first leg of their year-long 2012 world tour.

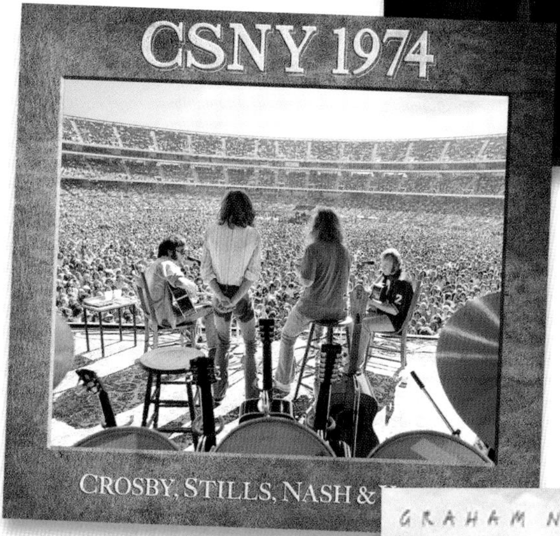

Left: *CNSY 1974* is a three-CD document of 1974's 'Doom Tour', carefully curated by Graham Nash. It would enter the top 20 in *Billboard's* album charts. (*Rhino*)

Right: *Over The Years*. Nash's 2018 'best of' album includes previously unheard demos of 'Pre-Road Downs', 'Teach Your Children', 'Our House', 'Just a Song Before I Go' and 'Wasted on the Way'.

Crosby…

Stills…

…and Nash in happier times.

CSN – as an active band – seem to be over (at time of writing) after a serious falling out between Crosby and the others in 2013-2014.

a new chorus and lose CSN's insipid harmonies and this might sound like something from, say, *Tonight's the Night*. Might.

'Don't Say Goodbye' (Nash / Vitale)

As usual, you cannot doubt Nash's sincerity here. 'Don't Say Goodbye' is piano-based and clear of much the glossy '80s production elsewhere on the album. Stephen Stills' growling, heavy-handed guitar solo doesn't fit the mood of the song at all, but in context of the of the rest of *American Dream*, 'Don't Say Goodbye' is a triumph. The live version from the 1988 Bridge School concerts is astounding.

'This Old House' (Young)

Released as a single, 1989. Did not chart.

Neil Young plays all of the instruments on this minor key country tune, first performed with his country band the International Harvesters in 1985. There are gallons of reverb all over everything – the chorus vocals are overpowering. Young's guitar picking is gorgeous, though, and the pump organ that colours the last chorus is lovely.

'Nighttime for the Generals' (Crosby / Doerge)

Released as a single, 1988. Highest chart position: 39 (US Mainstream Rock).

A clunky pissed-off rocker from Crosby– another song made almost unlistenable by over-production. An attempt to revisit Stills' and Young's guitar solo heroics of the past sounds forced. This so nearly a brilliant song, but what we have is a frustrating mush.

'Shadowland' (Ryan / Nash / Vitale)

Recorded in April 1987, several months before the concentrated album sessions the following Spring. It was co-written by long-time sideman Joe Vitale and by Rick Ryan, of whom very little is known. 'Shadowland' opens with rain effects, a shrill drum machine, plinking synthesiser and total lack of melody. The effect is to want to turn the song off within 60 seconds. If you get to the middle eight, then you'll enjoy the song completely disappearing down the pan.

Despite a typically poetic opening verse from Nash ('Behind a nation's blind salute / Behind 'my country `tis of thee' / Behind the pain that won't compute / Erase the memory'), 'Shadowland' is quite possibly the most horrible song ever released by CSNY.

'Drivin' Thunder' (Stills / Young)

Driving slide guitar opens this fast two-chord Stills blues-rocker. It could have been written in five minutes and sounds nothing at all like CSNY. Another version of this song is included on Stills' 2005 solo album *Man Alive!*

'Clear Blue Skies' (Nash)

'Clear Blue Skies', with its environmental message, had been in CSN's set for a few years and was tagged by Nash as a contender for the unreleased 1985 CSN album. This version can be heard on *Reflections*. The earlier rendition sounds cleaner and less forced– whilst not a classic, it's preferable to the CSNY version on *American Dream* where Nash's keening tenor and Crosby's strong harmony are lost amongst the production bustle.

'That Girl' (Stills / Vitale / Glaub)

Released as a single, 1989. Highest chart position: 25 (US Mainstream Rock).

A horns-driven R&B song which would sit quite well on a Stills solo album, but is out of place here.

'Compass' (Crosby)

Released as the b-side to 'American Dream', 1988.

David Crosby:

> A song about finding your way. I'm pissed at myself, deeply, for the 10 years – at least – of time that I wasted just getting smashed. That's really a waste. I'm supposed to be making music. I'm ashamed of that.

At last. We're three quarters through a disappointing album and here is a masterpiece, pure and simple.

Crosby's lowest point was in March 1986, when he entered the Texas Department of Corrections, in Huntsville, about 70 miles north of Houston. He had voluntarily surrendered to authorities in December 1985 after a series of drug and weapons-related misdemeanours. He kicked his habit in Texas. He was paroled on 8 August 1986 and was back on stage with Graham Nash on 22 August.

'I have wasted ten years in blindfold', he sings in 'Compass'. We believe him. 'When I saw the lyrics to 'Compass'', Crosby wrote in his autobiography, 'I realised that even though I was still suffering and things were not fun, there was obviously more of me awake that had been in a long time. It was the turning point.'

'Compass' shows just how brilliant David Crosby can be with the 'Guinnevere' tuning, the right song and the right arrangement. The odd tunings and time signatures, howling harmonica, shimmering harmonies, wide-open spaces and utterly sincere lead vocal performance from Crosby are peerless. And in the context of *American Dream*, 'Compass' shines brightly indeed.

Rolling Stone, however, didn't agree:

Unfortunately, American Dream's most cringe-inducing moment occurs at its point of greatest ambition. 'Compass' – Crosby's five-minute acoustic ballad of his struggle with addiction – is so strained in its effort to achieve poetry that it's more likely to generate laughter than sympathy. Gnarled lines like 'I have seized deaths door-handle / Like a fish out of water / Waiting for the mercy of the cat' argue the lingering effects of the drugs Crosby has so bravely kicked.

They're wrong.

'Soldiers of Peace' (Nash / Doerge / Vitale)

Graham Nash: 'A friend had been making a film about Vietnam veterans who were traveling to Nicaragua and talking with the soldiers there about the futility of war. They were pointing out to these soldiers how they had been lied to by their own government and ignored when they returned home. At the same time, David and I had been invited to play at a Vietnam Veterans benefit, and like many Americans we went to see the Vietnam Memorial. It makes most people who walk down it cry before they get halfway, and the reason is very simple: there are too many names on that wall. This song came out of these experiences.'

'Soldiers of Peace', despite its shiny, massive production, could have come from *Songs for Beginners* or *Wild Tales*. It makes a statement, has genuine dynamics and an uplifting chorus ('So come all you warriors who live for the fight / Come listen to somebody, someone who might / Have been there before you and they have the right / They've been dying to tell you the score / The old warriors don't want you to hurt any more'). Young's lead guitar cuts through everything.

Intriguingly, an orchestral version remains in the vaults.

'Feel Your Love' (Young)

And boom. Neil Young comes through with this quite beautiful, gentle love song– quiet and reflective with stopped acoustic guitar, subtle percussion and gorgeous singing. If the whole album had been half as good as this then it could sit amongst any of CSN(Y)'s other releases.

'Night Song' (Stills / Young)

The grand finale. The 'why not keep on singing' refrain, Young's backing vocals and some stinging guitar push through the muddy, keyboard-heavy, reverb-laden production. It's Stills' best song on the album, but that's not saying much. There is a less-cluttered version used on an episode of *The New Twilight Zone*, broadcast 11 October 1986.

How frustrating to have such second-rate material as 'Night Song', 'Name of Love', 'Shadowland' and 'Got It Made' on the same album as 'Don't Say Goodbye', 'Compass' and 'Feel Your Love'. *American Dream*. Remix, please.

Other contemporary songs considered for *American Dream*

'Count on Me' (Stills)
An outtake from the Spring 1988 sessions at Young's Redwood Digital studios.

'Dancing in the Streets' (Gaye / Hunter / Stevenson)
Yes, the Martha and the Vandellas song.

'Feel Your Love' (Stills / Nash)
An outtake from *Daylight Again* recorded 1982 and later released on the 2006 CD version. Presumably, two songs called 'Feel Your Love' was one too many.

'Game of Hearts' (Nash / Vitale)
An outtake from the Spring 1988 sessions at Young's Redwood Digital studios; recorded again for Crosby & Nash's abandoned 1989 album. It was recorded by Joellen Hoff on her 2016 album *Southern Comfort*.

'Hungry' (Stills)
An outtake from the Spring 1988 sessions at Young's Redwood Digital studios.

'You Might Be Loved' (Stills)
An unreleased song first recorded during sessions for *Daylight Again* and scheduled for release on the *As I Come of Age* album. Stills clearly was not done with the song as another version was recorded at Record One in Los Angeles in September 1988.

'Somewhere Somehow' (Nash)
Eventually renamed 'Love Lies Tonight' and recorded for *Songs for Survivors*.

'There Ain't Nothing Left' (Stills)
An outtake from the Spring 1988 sessions at Young's Redwood Digital studios.

'Tracks in the Dust' (Crosby)
One of Crosby's best songs, offered to CSNY but coolly received: either by Young or Stills as the released version, recorded in May 1988 for Crosby's *Oh Yes I Can* album, features Nash.

'Try to Find Me' (Nash)
This song was performed by Graham Nash many times as part of his solo set at CSN concerts between 1987 and 1992 but was overlooked for both *American Dream* and *Live it Up*. An acoustic version is on *The Acoustic Concert* DVD (1991). A solo recording from 2000 is included on the *Reflections* box set– it's quite lovely.

'White Line' (Young)
Recorded by Young and Crazy Horse for Ragged Glory in April 1990.

1990: Live It Up

Personnel:
David Crosby: vocals; electric guitar on 'Tomboy'
Stephen Stills: vocals; guitars on 'Live It Up','If Anybody Had a Heart','Tomboy', 'Haven't We Had Enough?','(Got to Keep) Open' and 'Straight Line'; keyboards on 'Tomboy'; bass on '(Got to Keep) Open'
Graham Nash: vocals; acoustic guitar on 'Tomboy' and'House of Broken Dreams' and
Tony Beard: percussion programming on 'Yours and Mine'; electric guitar on 'Straight Line'
Vince Charles: percussion on 'Arrows'
Craig Doerge: keyboards on 'If Anybody Had a Heart', 'Yours and Mine', 'Straight Line', 'House of Broken Dreams', 'Arrows' and 'After the Dolphin'
Bob Glaub: bass on 'Tomboy', 'Yours and Mine', 'Straight Line', and 'House of Broken Dreams'
Mike Fisher: percussion on 'If Anybody Had a Heart' and 'After the Dolphin'
Peter Frampton: guitar solo on 'Straight Line'
Bruce Hornsby: piano, accordion on '(Got to Keep) Open'
Michael Landau: guitar on 'If Anybody Had a Heart' and 'After the Dolphin'
Branford Marsalis: soprano saxophone on 'Yours and Mine' and 'Arrows'
Roger McGuinn: guitar on 'If Anybody Had a Heart'
Michito Sanchez: percussion on 'Tomboy' and '(Got to Keep) Open'
Leland Sklar: bass on 'If Anybody Had a Heart', 'Arrows', and 'After the Dolphin'
John David Southern: vocals on 'If Anybody Had a Heart'
Joe Vitale: drums; synthesizers on 'Live It Up','If Anybody Had a Heart','Tomboy','Yours and Mine','(Got to Keep) Open','House of Broken Dreams','Arrows' and 'After the Dolphin'; keyboards on 'Live It Up','If Anybody Had a Heart' and 'Yours and Mine'; organ on 'After the Dolphin'; percussion on 'Straight Line'
The Williams Family – vocals on 'Live It Up'
Recorded: February 1986 to April 1990 mostly at the Record Plant in Los Angeles. The recording dates for the individual tracks are: February 1986: 'Live It Up'; January 1989: 'If Anybody Had a Heart'; February 1989: 'After the Dolphin'; March 1989: 'Arrows'; January 1990: 'Tomboy', 'Straight Line', 'House of Broken Dreams'; February 1990: 'Haven't We Lost Enough', 'Yours and Mine'; April 1990: '(Got to Keep) Open'.
Produced by Crosby, Stills & Nash, Joe Vitale and Stanley Johnston.
Release date:26 June 1990 (US). Highest chart position: 57 (US). Did not chart in the UK.

Wait? What? Aren't Crosby, Stills and Nash songwriters as well as musicians? For their fourth studio album, we get co-writes with Craig Doerge, Michael Hedges and Kevin Cronin, and three songs on which none of the three principals has any writing credit whatsoever.

The album started as a fourth Crosby & Nash album, with 'Live It Up', 'If Anybody Had a Heart', 'After the Dolphin' and 'Arrows' all recorded during 1989 and retained. Stills joined the sessions in January 1990. Despite an over-slick, radio-friendly production, *Live It Up* has some good songs: Crosby's 'Yours and Mine' has lovely touches of jazzy sax from Branford Marsalis; 'House of Broken Dreams' is a minor Nash classic; Stills' 'Haven't We Lost Enough' was his best song for years. 'Tomboy', on the other hand…

Several famous guest musicians appear on the album: Peter Frampton, Bruce Hornsby, Michael Landau, Branford Marsalis, Roger McGuinn, John David Souther. None of these could rescue *Live It Up* from being the worst CSN studio album. 'The project was a little bit painful for me,' Graham Nash recalls. 'I produced the record with Joe Vitale and Stanley Johnson. And I found it very difficult to take a leadership role and maintain my friend/band vibe with David and Stephen. I couldn't separate myself.'

And then there is the truly horrendous album sleeve: hotdogs on the moon, anyone? You *can* judge an album by the cover — a free copy of *Illegal Stills* to anyone who can justify it.

Live It Up, with no hit singles, charted at no. 57 in the US. Having taken the 'chase chart success' career to its logical conclusion Crosby, Stills and Nash changed strategy in 1991 and 1992: touring for the first times as an acoustic trio, over 130 concerts, over 60 different songs. If CSN lost their identity in the 80s, then the 90s saw them getting back to what they did best.

'Live It Up' (Vitale)

Released as a single, 1990. B-side 'Chuck's Lament'. Highest chart position: 7 (US Mainstream Rock).

The album's lead-off song and single was written by and performed almost solely by Joe Vitale, CSN's drummer, keyboard player and occasional co-writer since 1977. Nash and Crosby's vocals were added during sessions for their planned duo album; Stills guitar and vocals were overdubbed much later. It's generic '80s rock.

'If Anybody Had a Heart' (Souther / Kortchmar)

Written by JD Souther and Danny Kortchmar, with a typically robust Souther melody. British rocker John Waite had recorded the song in 1986 for the soundtrack of the Rob Lowe / Demi Moore film *About Last Night*.

Nash was fond enough of this uninspired performance to include it on his *Reflections* box set. Beyond some jangly guitar from Roger McGuinn and a loud guitar solo from Stills, 'If Anybody Had a Heart' has very little to recommend it. Whisper it – John Waite's version is better.

'Tomboy' (Stills)

The opening electric sitar is the only point of interest in this tired, clunky, decidedly sexist Stills song with a limp reggae feel. The Crosby and Nash harmonies lift the choruses, if you haven't skipped the track before then.

'The single worst track Stills had released to date,' suggests Alan Pattinson.

'Haven't We Lost Enough?' (Stills / Cronin)

Wow. A fabulous acoustic song co-written with Kevin Cronin of REO Speedwagon.

Recalls Stephen Stills:

> Kevin and I were living in Encino, and in similar conditions romantically, that is, at the end of relationships. And while commiserating with each other one night, we decided to write a song. We finished it in the studio one night several years later and recorded it the next day. One of my best efforts in years. With acoustic music, there's no place to hide.

Twenty years after '4 + 20', Stills is once again vulnerable and needy. This time, Crosby and Nash add their characteristic harmonies and we have a song that sits comfortably next to CSN's other acoustic classics.

'Yours and Mine' (Doerge / Crosby / Nash)

A preachy song from Crosby, co-written with Graham Nash and Craig Doerge. Its jazz-tinged arrangement is a welcome contrast to the slick, '80s slush heard elsewhere on this album. It's tailor-made for CPR who performed it live in 2005.

David Crosby: 'The idea came from seeing the cover of *Time* magazine showing a twelve-year-old kid, proudly holding an AK-47 assault rifle. And I thought, 'How can we have gotten everything so wrong?''

Crosby wrote the words first and presented them to pianist Craig Doerge, co-author of 'Shadow Captain', 'Nighttime for the Generals' and others. Graham Nash rewrote the melody – the chorus, in particular, bears his stamp. CSN's chorus vocals are strong, and Branford Marsalis' sinuous saxophone winds around the melody.

'(Got to Keep) Open' (Stills / Nash)

An up-tempo and commercial song, with Cuban rhythms and hints of the Caribbean: perhaps a conscious attempt to revisit the steel drums of 'Love the One You're With'. '(Got to Keep) Open' was attempted for the abandoned 1978 follow-up to *CSN* and later planned to appear on Stills' unreleased 1979 solo album. Nash is credited as co-writer; presumably he wrote the bridge.

'Straight Line' (Beard)

A song written by drummer and songwriter Tony Beard who has worked with Go West, Bucks Fizz, Hall and Oates, Mike Oldfield and Roger Daltrey. It's very much in Nash's style. Peter Frampton plays the solo here, because, according to

Nash, Stills couldn't play over the chord changes. It's very commercial, with a nice Nash vocal, but is lightweight and forgettable with an antiseptic production.

'House of Broken Dreams' (Nash)

Another acoustic song, this one from Graham Nash. Very good it is, too: the antithesis of 'Our House', tracing the disillusionment when a relationship that started so well ('and everything is easy 'cos of you') turns sour ('separate houses, separate hearts / It's hard to face the feelings tearing us apart').

Nash wrote the song after calling his friend David Gilmour, whose first marriage was falling apart. A bitter Gilmour would answer 'hello, house of broken dreams'. The backing is subtle, modern without sounding overwhelming and Crosby's backing vocals ring out.

'Arrows' (Hedges / Crosby)

Back to *Whistling Down the Wire*-era Crosby and Nash, as Craig Doerge's familiar electric piano lays down that relaxed mid-70s feel. Soprano sax from Branford Marsalis adds further interest and Lee Sklar's sinuous bass playing sits beneath.

'After the Dolphin' (Nash / Doerge)

'I tried to write an anti-war statement,' says Graham Nash, 'and used the 1915 first bombing of a civilian target by an enemy aircraft. The German air force dropped a bomb on a pub in the East End of London called the Dolphin, and killed seven people.'

An epic song with a huge production, this is the only track on *Live it Up* to be sung in three-part harmony throughout. The lyrics are direct ('What will become of us all? / Who knows the story? / Will we witness the final fall / Of the hope and the glory?) and the anger in Crosby's voice is plain to hear. The lift as the song moves into its chorus is palpable.

A 4:35 edited version is on *Reflections*.

Other contemporary songs

'Chippin' Away' (Fedora)

A song from Nash's *Innocent Eyes* album with new vocals (including James Taylor) and guitar and bass from Stills added in 1989. This inoffensive light reggae song was performed by CSN at their impromptu performance at the Berlin Wall on 21 November 1989. Nash has told the story of how there was no PA, so they arranged to have the song broadcast on the local radio station– CSN sang along to hundreds of transistor radios. 'It probably seems odd that Americans would care that much,' Crosby said in 2013, 'but the Wall was an obscenity to us.'

'Chuck's Lament: A Child's Dream' (Crosby / Stills / Nash / Vitale)

The b-side of 'Live it Up', released as a single in 1990.

This was recorded in 1985-1986 and was played over the credits of the 1987 American sports drama film *Amazing Grace and Chuck*, directed by Mike Newell and starring Gregory Peck and Jamie Lee Curtis. It's the only CSN song which credits all three as co-composers. With a bit more work, this could have been a classic. David Crosby: 'It's a good song.' Under the '80s sheen, it is.

'Mystery' (Stills), **'Hungry'** (Stills), **'Standing Alone'** (Stills), **'A Bit About Love'** (Stills), **'Seas Like These'** (Nash)

Five songs from the *Live It Up* sessions that have yet to be released. It's hard to believe that none of these is better than 'Tomboy'. 'Hungry' was originally part of the *American Dream* sessions. 'Mystery', recorded with a string section, would be re-visited in 1997.

1994: After The Storm

Personnel:
David Crosby: vocals; acoustic guitar on 'Find a Dream' and 'After the Storm'
Stephen Stills: vocals; guitars all tracks except 'Street to Lean On' and 'After the Storm'; bass on 'Only Waiting for You' and 'It Won't Go Away'; piano on 'Only Waiting for You'
Graham Nash: vocals; acoustic guitar on 'Find a Dream', 'Unequal Love' and 'After the Storm'; harmonica on 'Find A Dream', 'Unequal Love' and 'In My Life'; piano on 'Find a Dream'
and
Lenny Castro: percussion on 'Only Waiting for You'
Jody Cortez: drums on 'Only Waiting for You'
Craig Doerge: keyboards on 'After the Storm'
Michael Finnigan: organ on 'Only Waiting for You', 'Till It Shines', 'It Won't Go Away', 'Street to Lean On' and 'Bad Boyz'; synthesizer, vocals on 'Only Waiting for You'
Daniel 'Freebo' Friedberg – bass on 'After the Storm'
Michael Hedges: guitar on 'Street to Lean On'
James 'Hutch' Hutchinson – bass on 'Find a Dream', 'Unequal Love', 'Till It Shines', 'These Empty Days' and 'Street to Lean On'
Tris Imboden: drums on 'Camera' and 'Panama'
Ethan Johns: drums on 'Find a Dream', 'Unequal Love', 'Till It Shines', 'These Empty Days', 'In My Life', 'Street to Lean On', 'Bad Boyz' and 'After the Storm'; percussion on 'Find a Dream', 'Unequal Love', 'Till It Shines', 'Bad Boyz' and 'After the Storm'; guitars on 'Find a Dream', 'Till It Shines', 'These Empty Days', 'Street to Lean On' and 'Bad Boyz'; mandocello on 'In My Life'
Rick Marotta: drums on 'It Won't Go Away' and 'Bad Boyz'
Rafael Padila: percussion on 'Camera' and 'Panama'
Joe Rotondi: keyboards on 'Panama'
Chris Stills: acoustic guitar on 'In My Life'; Spanish guitar on 'Panama'; piano on 'These Empty Days'
Jen Stills: backing vocals on 'After the Storm'
Alexis Sklarevski: bass on 'Camera', 'Bad Boyz' and 'Panama'
Benmont Tench: Hammond B-3 on 'Unequal Love'
Recorded: January 1994, Groove Masters, Santa Monica: 'Unequal Love', 'Till It Shines', 'These Empty Days';February 1994, Ocean Way Studios, Hollywood: 'Find a Dream'. 'Street to Lean On'; April-July 1994, O'Henry Sound Studios: 'Camera', 'It Won't Go Away', 'In My Life', 'Bad Boyz', 'After the Storm', 'Panama', 'Only Waiting for You'. Produced by Glyn Johns.
Released: 16 August 1994 (US). Highest chart position: 98 (US). Did not chart in the UK.

Crosby, Stills and Nash ditch the co-writers and unexpectedly come up with two-thirds of a really great album. Much of the credit must go to producer Glyn Johns, who has worked with the Rolling Stones, the Small Faces, Led Zeppelin,

the Beatles, Bob Dylan, the Band, the Who, the Eagles, Eric Clapton and many others. He had mixed *Songs for Beginners* in 1971 and produced Crosby's *Thousand Roads* in 1993. '[*After the Storm*] came about because we had cut a couple of tracks with Crosby for a solo album at my studio in England,' Johns noted in his memoirs. 'It resulted in my son Ethan going on the road with them for the next year, with Graham Nash keeping a fatherly eye on him.'

This was the first CSN project that started and finished as a CSN project since 1977's *CSN*. It was their best collection of new songs, alone or together, since *Daylight Again*, twelve years before. The album was released almost exactly twenty-five years after CSN's appearance at the Woodstock festival, which cannot have been a coincidence. To promote the album, Crosby, Stills and Nash played almost one hundred concerts and appeared on both *The Tonight Show with Jay Leno* and *Late Night with David Letterman*. Atlantic did little in the way of promotion, which contributed both to low sales and CSN departing their long-term record label a few year later.

Stephen Stills: 'The old spirit of collaboration is back. And it's high time, too. There are so many old wounds that have sometimes gotten in the way. But this year it's been really cool.'

'Only Waiting for You' (Stills)

An upbeat, positive, joyous pop song, a rewrite of 'Dark Star' for Stills' soon-to-be third wife Kristen. They would marry in 1996. The first verse has some truly terrible lyrics: 'I cannot remember feeling quite so self-assured / It must have been back in my teens. / I was such a basket case when I was young / It's obviously something that I dreamed.' The last verse, however, is bang on the money: 'I've got one last truly great love left in my life / And my heart is tellin' me it might be you. / So forget your disappointments, I'll forget about my past / I was really only waiting for you.' Wonderful!

The harmonies shine out in the chorus and Stills plays piano, bass and guitar: everything except drums and some keyboards. In the context of a 1994 CSN album this is a strong song. It was the last song recorded for the album.

'Find a Dream' (Nash)

'Find a Dream' has a gorgeous, sparse subtle production, which sounds a lot like mid-'70s Neil Young. Even Stills' guitar break echoes CSN's fourth limb. Nash sings lead with Crosby and Stills alternating on harmony for the verses.

If Nash's 'curtain / uncertain' rhyme sounds familiar, it's because he had used it on 'Be Yourself' on his first solo album, *Songs for Beginners*. Here he nearly reverses the analogy.

In 1971: 'Your life seems uncertain / So you draw the curtain / Pretending there's nobody home.'

In 2004: 'Life is uncertain, life is unknown / Life is a shot in the dark / Life is a curtain, always unfolding / Life is an ember and a spark.'

A lost gem.

'Camera' (Crosby / Stills)
A rare Crosby / Stills co-write: Crosby wrote the lyrics ('I rode my bike to town today, wobbling down the path, I knew the kids would see me, I love it when they laugh') and both are credited with the music.

The song's brief chorus seems to be flown in from a different song together: 'Wish I were a camera / I wish it all the time / It gives my eyes a reason / It gives my life a rhyme'

The instrumentation has a Latin feel and combines acoustic guitar flourishes with busy drums, courtesy of Chicago's drummer Tris Imboden, lots of percussion and bassist Alexis Sklarevski who toured with the band in 1994.

'Unequal Love' (Nash)
One of Graham Nash's heartfelt acoustic ballads, beautifully produced with understated instrumental backing and some subtle electric guitar from Stills. The song features tasteful washes of organ from Benmont Tench and harmonica solos from Graham Nash. Lovely.

'Till It Shines' (Crosby)
The first flowering of Crosby's forthcoming renaissance with CPR is heard in this album highlight. Crosby strips down the music and lyrics to uncomplicated blues-based verses with forceful vocal leads. A pulsating breakdown with Stills' lyrical guitar and Michael Finnegan's trilling organ drive the song along. The live version on *Live at Cuesta College* (1998) is highly recommended.

'It Won't Go Away' (Stills)
A tightly-produced, up-tempo Stills song. Session drummer Rick Marotta keeps the arrangement moving. It started life as a bluesy acoustic song on CSN's 1992 tour– the almost stream-of-consciousness lyrics target crooked politicians and media: 'Somebody wants us divided / Someone of evil intent / Trying to confuse and control / The minds of the innocent'. Nash's tenor leavens the sometimes-awkward lyrical content.

'These Empty Days' (Nash / Crosby)
A rare Crosby / Nash co-write, sung by all three together with vocal breaks by Stills. The middle eight sounds likes Crosby's work, the verses are pure Nash. It's pleasant enough, and beautifully produced, but not much more than filler.

'In My Life' (Lennon / McCartney)
Stephen Stills had recorded this Beatles song on his *Stills Alone* album (1991). This stately, gorgeous, exposed arrangement adds harmonica, brushed drums and mandocello. And Crosby and Nash's impeccable harmonies, of course.

'Street to Lean On' (Crosby)

A snappy, funky Crosby song. It's musically excellent, but the lyrics are preachy and tired: 'Bag lady's complainin' / To the cop on the beat / She says she's got nowhere to go / She got nothin' to eat'. The sparkling acoustic guitar is provided by the late Michael Hedges, an awesome musician who worked on two of the best songs on Crosby's *Oh Yes I Can* and was paid tribute in song on the 2004 Crosby & Nash album.

'Bad Boyz' (Stills)

The final three songs on *After the Storm* feel like an afterthought. 'Bad Boyz' is an unconvincing bluesy, shuffling Stills 4/4 rocker, with loud electric guitars, trite lyrics and not much to recommend a second listen. 'Voodoo Chile' it ain't, even though it would like to be.

'After the Storm' (Nash)

A loping acoustic folk waltz. It has some strong lyrics, lovely chord changes, a terrific lead vocal from Nash and strong backing from Stills. The beautiful high falsetto vocal, clearly audible in the second verse and hugely effective on 'I needed a friend' and 'lingering on', is by Stills' daughter Jennifer. 'After the Storm' is a gorgeous song that offers little new but shows the high level of craft employed on this final CSN studio album.

'Panama' (Stills)

A tired re-tread of the Cuban rhythms we'd heard from Stills on 'Pensiamento', 'Guaguancó de Veró', 'Turn Back the Pages', 'Soldier', '50/50' and the closing section of 'Suite: Judy Blue Eyes'. This dull song provides a flat ending to an otherwise high-quality, if hardly groundbreaking, new album.

Other contemporary songs

'Rusty and Blue' (Crosby), **'Somehow She Knew'** (Crosby)

Two excellent David Crosby songs, supposedly recorded by CSN in February 1994. They were certainly recorded by CPR three years later. 'Somehow She Knew' was originally called 'The Fisher King Song' and was part of Crosby's solo section of CSN concerts for years before he recorded it.

'Isn't It So' (Stills), **'Treetop Flyer'** (Stills)

Two songs from *Stills Alone*, re-recorded by CSN in March 1994 but so far unreleased. 'Treetop Flyer' dates from at least 1975. 'Isn't It So' was dropped in favour of 'Only Waiting for You'.

'Flipper (Main Title)' (Colcord / McNeely)

Alarmingly, this sappy film theme was the last-ever new studio release from Crosby, Stills and Nash. It's the title music to 1996 Alan Shapiro film featuring a pre-Frodo Elijah Wood.

CSN ba-da-di-dum along to the London Symphony Orchestra. The film was a big hit, so it's possible that this one song is has been heard by more casual listeners than any other CSN recording. It's great to hear CSN backed by a full orchestra, though. How amazing would it have been to hear those three voices backed by strings and brass? Other than this, we'll never know.

1999: Looking Forward

Personnel:
David Crosby; vocals; electric guitar on 'Stand and Be Counted'; acoustic guitar on 'Dream for Him'
Stephen Stills: vocals; guitars all tracks except 'Slowpoke', 'Out of Control' and 'Sanibel'; Hammond B-3, bass guitar, percussion on 'Faith in Me'; maracas, double bass on 'No Tears Left'; percussion on 'Queen of Them All'
Graham Nash: vocals; acoustic guitar on 'Someday Soon'
Neil Young: vocals; guitars all tracks except 'Sanibel'; harmonica on 'Slowpoke'; tiple on 'Out of Control'; celeste on 'Queen of Them All'
and
Alex Acuña: timbales on 'Faith in Me'
Lenny Castro: percussion on 'Heartland'
Vince Charles: percussion on 'Sanibel'
Luis Conte: congas, jombe bass drum, batas on 'Faith in Me'; percussion on 'Dream for Him'
Craig Doerge: keyboards on 'Sanibel'
Donald Dunn: bass on 'Looking Forward', 'Stand and Be Counted', 'Seen Enough', 'Slowpoke', 'Out of Control', 'Someday Soon' and 'Queen of Them All'
Michael Finnigan – Hammond B-3 on 'Stand and Be Counted', 'Heartland', 'No Tears Left' and 'Queen of Them All'
Snuffy Garrett: guitars on 'Sanibel'
Bob Glaub: bass on 'Sanibel'
James 'Hutch' Hutchinson – bass on 'Dream for Him'
Ben Keith: pedal steel guitar on 'Looking Forward', 'Slowpoke' and 'Out of Control'; Dobro on 'Looking Forward'
Jim Keltner: drums on 'Looking Forward', 'Slowpoke' and 'Out of Control'
Gerald Johnson: bass on 'Heartland'
Joe Lala: congas on 'Faith in Me'
Spooner Oldham: keyboards on 'Slowpoke' and 'Queen of Them All'; pump organ on 'Looking Forward'
James Raymond: piano on 'Heartland' and 'Dream for Him'
Denny Sarokin: guitars on 'Sanibel'
Joe Vitale: drums all tracks except 'Looking Forward', 'Slowpoke' and 'Out of Control'; Hammond B-3, batas on 'Faith in Me'
Recorded: November 1996 to July 1999 at Ga Ga's Room, Los Angeles, Conway Recording Studios, Hollywood, Ocean Studios, Burbank and Redwood Digital, Woodside. Produced by David Crosby, Stephen Stills, Graham Nash, Neil Young, Joe Vitale, Ben Keith, Stanley Johnston.
Release date: 26 October 1999 (US). Highest chart positions: 26 (US), 54 (UK).

CSNY's third and last studio album does not reach the heights of *Déjà Vu*. Thankfully, neither does it trawl the depths of *American Dream*, but it's a close call. If *American Dream* had three or four good songs, then *Looking Forward*

has perhaps five.

Looking Forward has the most convoluted history of any albums in the CSN / CSNY discography. Crosby, Stills and Nash terminated their contract with Atlantic and had begun to record new tracks out of their own pockets. Meanwhile, Stills and Young were working together on a Buffalo Springfield box set, eventually released in 2001. Stills played Young some of the new CSN recordings for a proposed album *Heartland*. Neil liked what he heard, especially Stills' 'Acadienne', and was impressed that they were paying their own expenses: that CSN were serious about making new music. Thus, Neil Young entered the project. And then, inevitably, took it over.

New songs written by Crosby, Stills and Nash, but none by Young, were recorded between November 1998 and February 1999 at Conway Recording Studios, Hollywood. Meanwhile, five finished songs from Young's as-yet-unreleased *Silver and Gold* album would have CSN vocals added in March 1999. Thus was the album pieced together. By April 1999, the tentative track listing was 'Stand and Be Counted', 'Looking Forward', 'Acadienne', 'Half Your Angels', 'Out Of Control', 'Heartland', 'Slowpoke', 'Dream For Him', 'Faith In Me', 'Try To Find Me', 'No Tears Left', 'Isn't It So', 'Morrison' and 'Mystery'. An old CSN version of Denny Sarokin's 'Sanibel' was retrieved from the *Live it Up* sessions and polished up at this time but wasn't added to the album's running order. Yet.

There were more sessions at Neil's instigation in May 1999, once again at Conway. Four new songs were recorded, although only two of these, 'Seen Enough' and 'Climber', were included in the album's proposed running order. *Heartland*, as it was then called, was mastered and ready for a July 1999 release and now included 'Faith In Me', 'Looking Forward', 'Heartland', 'Seen Enough', 'Climber', 'Isn't It So', 'Slowpoke', 'No Tears Left', 'Half Your Angels', 'Out Of Control', 'Stand and be Counted' and 'Sanibel'.

But Neil Young wasn't finished meddling. Everyone went back to his ranch to record three more new songs in July: 'Someday Soon', 'Queen of Them All' and 'Coming to the Rescue'. The tracklisting was revised to what we now know as *Looking Forward*. There's a good argument that each iteration was less interesting than the previous. In the end, only three songs survived from the unreleased 1998 CSN album to the final 1999 CSNY album, released on Young's long-term record label Reprise.

Young's songs, in particular hardly measure up to his other great songs of the 90s: a decade that had seen the release of *Ragged Glory*, *Harvest Moon, Sleeps with Angels* and *Broken Arrow*. They don't even measure up to the best CSN songs that were recorded for and dropped from *Looking Forward*: 'Morrison', 'Climber', 'Acadienne', 'Lost Another One', 'Half Your Angels' and 'Try to Find Me'.

> [This] album crosses the line separating eclectic and schizophrenic. It captures little of the passion and innovation that made Crosby, Stills, Nash and Young such an evocative voice for their generation.
>
> Carla Mastraccio, *The Crimson*, 29 October 1999

> Right, you knew already. But though I pray I hear solo Y render the title song hopeful instead of smug, I know that in my head I'll still hear N harmonising insipidly behind. And when S explains how when he was young, old people were wrong and now that he's old young people are wrong and then disses 'overfed talking heads' without ever once acknowledging overfed singing exhead C to his immediate left, I imagine some computer nerd with more brains than sense joining the arms race just to get even. Still a menace – and still conceited about it.
> Robert Christgau, *Village Voice*, 1999

'Faith in Me' (Stills / Vitale)
A cluttered, raucous production of another of Stills' percussion-laden Latin songs with a huge and simplistic chorus 'Have some faith in me / 'Cos we really do know better / And we do belong together'. It sounds tired and contrived.

'Looking Forward' (Young)
A laid-back country/folk song, not so far from 'Human Highway', but not as good, despite Nash's and Stills' tight harmonies and a beautiful production. Stills added his guitar to the completed Young master.

'Stand and Be Counted' (Crosby / Raymond)
Stills and Young rock out in a genteel and polite fashion on twin lead guitars. Stills' guitar is drenched in reverb and chorus effects and is mixed low in the left channel. Young, right channel, is playing his Gretch by the sounds of it. Crosby would announce this as a 'pissed-off rocker' on the band's 2000 tour. This version suggests nothing more than mild irritation.

'Heartland' (Nash)
Sung by Nash, with Crosby and Stills trading harmony lines on the verses, 'Heartland' builds to an uplifting chorus. Young's guitar pierces the CSN smoothness. A 2008 remix is included on *Reflections*.

'Seen Enough' (Stills)
A tough country blues, with the vocal melody, erm, borrowed from Bob Dylan's 'Subterranean Homesick Blues'. It's a shame he didn't nick the lyrics as well. His own are simply embarrassing. Sample: 'I lost my innocence over intolerance / All the indignities heaped on the black man / We went to church they all prayed for the white man / The cops and the preachers / Were most of 'em in the Klan? / What's a kid s'posed to think when the adults / Are all such hypocrites impossibly smug?'. The track itself, with Duck Dunn's bubbling bass and shimmering electric slide guitar, is great, as is Stills singing. Just don't listen to the words.

'Slowpoke' (Young)
'Slowpoke' drops the pace and draws a lot of momentum out of the album. It cops the opening rhythm from 'Heart of Gold', if not the same chords exactly– that drop to E minor at the end of each is identical though. It's a warm song, typical of Young's '90s acoustic work. CSN's chorus backing vocals are sweet but sound very much after-the-fact.

'Dream for Him' (Crosby)
A terrific jazzy rock song from CPR's album *Live at the Wiltern*, recorded in November 1998 and released about a month before *Looking Forward*. ''Dream for Him' was written to and for my son Django,' says Crosby. 'Having kids is the most important thing we get to do, and the most fun thing in your life, if you're lucky.'

His other son, James Raymond, guests on piano and adds some genuine sonic interest. Neil Young's subtle lead guitar underpins the song. Crosby's warm, controlled lead vocal brings out some vivid imagery: 'I want a world where I can tell him the truth / About everyone from Jesus to John Wilkes Booth.' A tremendous live CSNY version from 2002 is on *Voyage* (2006).

'No Tears Left' (Stills)
Released as a single, 1999. Highest chart position: 34 (US Mainstream Rock).

A standard Stills rocker with a bluesy bounce and cascading backing vocals. A live version from the Fillmore Auditorium, San Francisco, 14 September 1997 is available on the 2013 box set *Carry On*.

'Out of Control' (Young)
An excellent Young song, written his classic early-'70s style with shifting dynamics, distant pedal steel guitar and a tinkling upright piano. The lyrics are banal, though – surely the lines 'Once on a hill / There was a song / Nothing was wrong / That's when time stood still.' Are these just a first draft?

CSN are barely audible.

'Someday Soon' (Nash)
A simple, heartfelt and optimistic Graham Nash song, from the last batch of recording sessions. It's mostly acoustic– Nash's only credit on the instrument here – with a fabulous middle-eight which match Stills and Nash in great voice. The production is kept simple and effective.

'Queen of Them All' (Young)
A horrendous song, the last recorded for the album after *twenty* others had been rejected. It sounds like it was written and recorded in ten minutes. What were they thinking?

'Sanibel' (Sarokin)

An odd one, this. Recorded in 1990 during the Crosby & Nash sessions that preceded *Live it Up*, and polished in the first band sessions for *Looking Forward*, it's a rare Nash / Young duet: Nash sings the first verse, Young the second, Crosby and Nash sing the chorus. The song was written by Nashville-based guitar tutor and songwriter Denny Sarokin who plays guitar with famed musak record producer Snuff Garrett. As far as I can tell, none of CSNY perform musically on this track. I mean, it's quite pleasant, but why?

Other contemporary songs

'Climber' (Crosby)

Recorded during the May 1999 sessions for *Looking Forward* but not used. The CSNY version was released on the *Voyage* box set in 2006. By then, Crosby had recorded it again, for his second album with CPR, but its exclusion from *Looking Forward* is an outrage. It would have been a highlight of the album. Some sources list a Nash song called 'Up the Wall' as dating from these sessions– this may well be a misidentification of 'Climber'.

'Good to See You' (Young)

Recorded by Young for *Silver and Gold*, released in April 2000. CSNY's version has not been heard.

'Silver and Gold' (Young)

Worked up with CSN harmonies for *Looking Forward* but if it was recorded by CSNY, it remains unreleased. Young released it in 2000 as the title track of his 23rd solo album.

'Wounded World' (Stills / Nash)

Later released on *Man Alive!,* Nash sings harmonies on Stills' solo version, so it's possible that this is an outtake from the *Looking Forward* sessions.

2006: Déjà Vu Live

Personnel:
David Crosby: vocals, rhythm guitar
Stephen Stills: vocals, guitars, keyboards
Graham Nash: vocals, rhythm guitar, piano
Neil Young: vocals, guitars, piano
and
Tom Bray: trumpet
Chad Cromwell: drums
Ben Keith: pedal steel guitar
Spooner Oldham: keyboards
Rick Rosas: bass
Recorded in 2006 on CSNY's US tour. Produced by Neil Young and LA Johnson.
Released 22 July 2008. Highest chart positions: 153 (US), did not chart in the UK.

CSNY's first tour for twenty-six years started in New York on 4 April 2000. Through the forty-five dates of the tour, they played forty different songs and were often on stage for three hours or more. The opening electric set typically opened with 'Carry On' and included the vintage 'Southern Man', 'Pre-Road Downs', '49 Bye-Byes', 'Marrakesh Express', 'Almost Cut My Hair' and 'Cinnamon Girl', as well as a sprinkling of newer songs such as 'Stand and Be Counted', 'Heartland', 'Slowpoke' and 'Faith in Me'. An hour-long acoustic set would inevitably roll out the venerable 'Helplessly Hoping', 'Our House', 'Old Man', 'After The Goldrush', 'Guinnevere', 'Love the One You're With' and 'Teach Your Children', with new songs such as 'Dream For Him', 'Someday Soon', 'Looking Forward', Out of Control' and 'Seen Enough'. A rocking third set combined 'Woodstock', 'Long Time Gone', 'Ohio', 'For What It's Worth' and 'Down by the River' with a lengthy workout on Young's 'Rockin' in the Free World'. 'Long May You Run' was an appropriate encore. CNSY were backed by Jim Keltner and Donald 'Duck' Dunn after long-time CSN side-men Joe Vitale and Michael Finnigan were sacked at Young's insistence. Graham Nash:

> It was very tough to let Vitale and Michael Finnigan go; they've been part of our band for 20-odd years. And it was very tough; personally, it was very, very hard to make that call. But musically, I understand completely. And within a week, Neil had been proven right. We needed space. When you bring a Neil Young guitar into a band, you better be able to hear it ... So it was a very tough call. I believe they took it with the spirit in which it was meant. It was not personal; it was purely musical. And once again, Neil's instincts were correct.

The tour was repeated in 2002, another forty-one dates in total. It was the ninth best-grossing US tour of the year. The set-list was more diverse, dropping most of the *Looking Forward* songs and adding new or newish songs from Young ('Going Home', 'Two Old Friends' and 'You're My Girl'), Stills ('Feed the

People') and Nash ('Half Your Angels'), thrilling takes on 'I Used to Be a King', 'Cinnamon Girl' and 'Carry Me', and sometimes a surprising and very effective version of 'Eight Miles High'. Live takes of Crosby's 'Dream for Him' and Stills' rendition of Otis Redding's 'Ole Man Trouble' are on the box sets *Voyage* and *Carry On* respectively. The additional musicians on this tour were Booker T Jones (keyboards), Donald 'Duck' Dunn (bass) and Steve 'Smokey' Potts (drums).

A double-headed CSNY / Eagles tour of Europe for 2004 was planned but did not go ahead.

CSNY's three-month, 35-date 2006 'Freedom of Speech' tour was a tiger of a different stripe. The majority of Young's challenging album *Living with War* comprised around a quarter of the set. All sets would begin with Young's 'Flags of Freedom' and a typical show would include 'Carry On', 'Wooden Ships', 'Long Time Gone', 'Military Madness', 'After the Garden', 'Living With War', 'The Restless Consumer', 'Shock and Awe', 'Wounded World', 'Almost Cut My Hair', 'Immigration Man', 'Families' and 'Déjà Vu'. A second set included 'Helplessly Hoping', 'Our House', 'Only Love Can Break Your Heart', 'Guinnevere', 'Milky Way Tonight', 'Treetop Flyer', 'Roger and Out', 'Southbound Train', 'Ole Man Trouble' 'Carry Me', 'Southern Cross' and 'Find the Cost of Freedom'. The first encore might include 'Teach Your Children', 'Let's Impeach the President', 'For What It's Worth', 'Chicago', 'Ohio' and 'What Are Their Names?'. The evening would usually close with 'Rockin' in the Free World'. Other songs performed on the tour included 'Woodstock', Stills' 'Feed the People' and 'Love the One You're With', and Young's 'From Hank to Hendrix', and 'Lookin' for a Leader'.

2008's *Déjà Vu Live* is a mixture of classics, songs from *Living with War* and an unexpected exhumation of a David Crosby album track. iTunes shoppers were treated to a bonus track: Young's 'The Restless Consumer'. The backing band were all familiar Young luminaries: Ben Keith (pedal steel), Spooner Oldham (keyboards), Rick Rosas (bass), Chad Cromwell (drums) and Tom Bray of the Blue Notes on trumpet. Young's dominance is complete. As Stills comments on the accompanying DVD, 'I'm in two minds about this whole thing.'

A contemporary DVD, confusingly called *Déjà Vu*, isn't a concert film, as surely most fans wanted to see, but a documentary directed by Neil Young and narrated by Mike Cerre a foreign correspondent for *ABC News Nightline*, where he earned an Emmy Award for his embedded reporting in the Iraq war of 2003 onwards. There are tantalising glimpses of CSNY on stage, performing powerful and loud versions of songs such as 'Military Madness' and 'Immigration Man', with all four singing and playing together.

We'll just have to resort to the bootleg albums to hear more, I guess.

'What Are Their Names?' (Crosby)

The sing-along track from side two of David Crosby's 1971 solo album *If I*

Could Only Remember My Name, most often played as the final song of the first encore. It's effectively placed as a rabble-rousing opening here.

'Living with War' (Young)

A piano-based instrumental theme tune with some guitar feedback.

'After the Garden' (Young)

A gruff, mid-paced rocker, with all four singers chanting the simple lyrics.

'Military Madness' (Nash)

A very loud, raucous version of Nash's highlight from *Songs for Beginners*. Young's voice is loud and clear in the chorus, and Spooner Oldham's bar-room piano tinkles along. And then Neil throttles Old Black, ladling white noise over this simple song.

'Let's Impeach the President' (Young)

A hilarious song, especially after the 2020 Trump impeachment trial. They sound old and grumpy here on lines such as 'What if Al Qaeda blew up the levees? / Would New Orleans have been safer that way? / Sheltered by our government's protection / Or was someone just not home that day?'

Many Republican fans walked out during this song. But for the wrong reasons.

'Déjà Vu' (Crosby)

A song that, despite its pedigree and quality, sounds quite out of place here. It's a tough arrangement, however, with Crosby and Nash in great voice, some roaring Stills lead guitar and Neil revisiting his fat Blue Tones guitar sound.

'Shock and Awe' (Young)

Within the context of *Living with War*, this is a terrific song. But within a CSNY arena concert tour it's uncompromising and mis-placed.

'Families' (Young)

My mother always said that if I couldn't write anything nice about something, then I shouldn't say anything. It's short though, at least.

'Wooden Ships' (Crosby / Kantner / Stills)

'Don't eat the brown acid!' quips Graham Nash before CSNY launch into their hippy anthem. Crosby and Nash sing the opening lines, not Stills and Crosby. Stills playing is decidedly wobbly and you can hear him grunting away in the chorus. It's nice to hear Neil Young play guitar on this song– he had played organ on the 1969 and 1974 tours.

'Looking for a Leader' (Young)

This song is just a riff with half-assed lyrics. 'Maybe it's Obama but he thinks that he's too young. Maybe it's Colin Powell, to right what he's done wrong.'

It's tempting to pretend this song simply doesn't exist.

'For What It's Worth' (Stills)

A revisit of Stills' first success a writer and his only lead vocal here: it's pretty good but very much a re-tread of past glories.

'Living with War' (Young)

The blaring trumpet offers something new, but CSN do not sound remotely engaged here.

'Roger and Out' (Young)

Blasts of Young's massive guitar smother a half-decent song that would probably work better acoustically. Or perhaps that would reveal its origins as a turgid rewrite of 'Knockin' on Heaven's Door'. This is one song too many from *Living with War*, frankly; a difficult album that does merit a close listen, especially in its 'raw' version. But it has absolutely nothing to do with CSNY.

'Find the Cost of Freedom' (Stills)

A guy in the crowd shouts 'yes!' as this song begins. Who can blame him after song after song of Young's tedious preaching? The harmonies are shaky, but the power of this song is undiminished, especially when Stills drops in a few riffs from 'Daylight Again'.

'Teach Your Children' (Nash)

Inevitably.

'Living with War' (Young)

A reprise of the piano theme. This time without the guitar feedback.

There's no disguising what this is: this is a set of ageing hippies lamenting the way things are now by connecting to who they were back then, reuniting for the new songs and mixing up relevant older ones – including, yes, the warhorses 'For What It's Worth' and 'Teach Your Children' – to provide a bridge to the past. CSNY don't run from their age, as they can't escape it: some voices have grown gravelly, the harmonies are shakier, there isn't quite as much muscle to the guitar. But by not running from these signs of age, CSNY wind up with a live album that has a bit of resonance, as when it's contrasted with the rangy, restless 4 Way Street, it's hard not to be a little moved and marvel that the band members feel so comfortable here, especially considering their tortured history.

This winds up being the overarching impression left by Déjà Vu Live, as despite the topicality of the set list, Déjà Vu Live feels curiously isolated; there may have been controversy on the tour, all chronicled on Young's film, but it doesn't feel engaged with the culture at large, which could be a side effect of the digital dislocation of the 21st century, or it could be a sign that CSNY are growing older and simply don't stir things up the way they did back then. But for those who are listening, their message has resonance -- and so does the music, as this live record winds up being a nice, understated grace note to their tumultuous career.
Stephen Thomas Erlewine. *Allmusic.com*, July 2008

And, with that, we've reached the end of CSN(Y)'s new album releases. It seems very unlikely that we'll see any more. What a long, strange trip it's been.

Compilation Albums, Archive Collections And Other Live Releases

Celebration Copy

Released: 1971 (US). Highest chart position: did not chart.

This was the first CSNY compilation album: a twelve-track promo released by Atlantic in 1971. It comprised six solo tracks and six band cuts: 'Love the One You're With' (Stephen Stills); 'Music Is Love' (David Crosby); 'Military Madness' (Graham Nash); 'Bluebird Revisited' (Stephen Stills); 'Simple Man' (Graham Nash); 'Orleans' (David Crosby); 'Long Time Gone' (Crosby, Stills & Nash); 'Marrakesh Express' (Crosby, Stills & Nash); 'Carry On' (Crosby, Stills, Nash & Young); 'Woodstock' (Crosby, Stills, Nash & Young); 'Teach Your Children' (Crosby, Stills, Nash & Young); 'Ohio' (Crosby, Stills, Nash & Young).

So Far

Released: 19 August 1974 (US). Highest chart position: 1 (US), 25 (UK).

So Far was an official album released mid-way through CSNY's US tour in Summer 1974. A 'best of' after just two albums? Record label cash-in ahoy!

Graham Nash: 'We were totally against *So Far* coming out.'

Of course, it's fabulous, and for twenty years was the only place to get 'Find the Cost of Freedom' without tracking down the 7" single of 'Ohio'. But no room for 2 minutes, 38 seconds of 'Marrakesh Express'...

Track-list: 'Déjà Vu', 'Helplessly Hoping', 'Wooden Ships', 'Teach Your Children', 'Ohio', 'Find the Cost of Freedom', 'Woodstock', 'Our House', 'Helpless', 'Guinnevere', 'Suite: Judy Blue Eyes'.

Replay

Released: 8 December 1980 (US). Highest chart position: 122 (US). Did not chart in the UK.

A second 'best of' after just three albums? Another record label cash-in! *Replay* adds three Stills solo songs to four from *CSN* and throws in 'Marrakesh Express' and 'Pre-Road Downs' from the debut album, a remix of 'Carry On' and one track from Crosby & Nash's *Wind on the Water*.

This is the only place to get the beefed-up version of 'Carry On', so if you're a completist, you need this. This remix/edit was released as single in 1980 (b / w 'Shadow Captain') but did not chart.

Track-list: 'Carry On' (1980 remix), 'Marrakesh Express', 'Just a Song Before I Go', 'First Things First', 'Shadow Captain', 'To the Last Whale...', 'Love the One You're With', 'Pre-Road Downs', 'Change Partners', 'I Give You Give Blind' (1980 remix), 'Cathedral'.

CSN [box set]

Released: 30 September 1991 (US). Highest chart position: 109 (US). Did not chart in the UK.

Eric Clapton's career-spanning *Crossroads* box set released 1988, and the advent of the CD enabled record companies to persuade fans to re-buy their record collections, sometimes enticed by unreleased songs. *Crossroads* sold more than four million copies worldwide and was presented with six awards, including two Grammies in 1989.

Box sets do their best to please everyone. But do the hardcore fans want to re-buy dozens of songs they already own? Does the casual fan want several rarities or just the hits? Of the CSN box set's 77 tracks, 25 had been unreleased previously, although many of these were alternate takes, alternate mixes, or concert versions of previously issued songs. Hardcore fans were rewarded with around one hundred minutes of unheard music: 'Suite: Judy Blue Eyes' (deleted drum track restored, alternative vocals), 'Helplessly Hoping' (CSNY 1969 rehearsal), 'You Don't Have to Cry' (1968 recording), 'Guinnevere' (Crosby demo), 'Blackbird' (1969 outtake), 'Almost Cut My Hair' (unedited take of track on *Déjà Vu*), 'Horses Through a Rainstorm' (*Déjà Vu*outtake), '4+20' (remix), 'Woodstock' (remix), 'The Lee Shore' (Déjà Vu outtake with 1991 vocal overdubs), 'Man in the Mirror' (live version, 1970), 'Black Queen' (live version, 1970), 'See the Changes' (CSNY 1973 version), 'Homeward Through the Haze' (CSNY 1974 version), 'Taken at All' (CSNY 1976 version), 'Dear Mr. Fantasy' (1980 Stills & Nash version), 'Got It Made' (1989 live version), 'As I Come of Age' (CSN 1981 remake), 'Soldiers of Peace' (remix). Each of these is mentioned in the appropriate chapter of this book.

The rest of the set includes from *Crosby, Stills & Nash*: 'Wooden Ships', 'Marrakesh Express', 'Long Time Gone', 'Lady of the Island'; from *Déjà Vu*: 'Teach Your Children', 'Déjà Vu', 'Helpless', 'Carry On / Questions', 'Our House'; from single: 'Ohio', 'Find the Cost of Freedom'; from *CSN*: 'In My Dreams', 'Just a Song Before I Go', 'Shadow Captain', 'Cathedral'' 'Cold Rain'; from *Daylight Again*: 'Wasted on the Way', 'Southern Cross', 'Daylight Again', 'Delta'; from *Allies*: 'Dark Star'; from *Live It Up*: 'Yours and Mine', 'Haven't We Lost Enough?', 'After the Dolphin'. Crosby solo: 'Laughing', 'Music Is Love', 'I'd Swear There Was Somebody Here', 'Tracks in the Dust', 'Drive My Car' (1978 version). Stills solo: 'Love the One You're With', 'Old Times Good Times', 'Change Partners', 'My Love Is a Gentle Thing' (previously unreleased), 'Word Game', 'Johnny's Garden', 'So Begins the Task', 'Turn Back the Pages', 'It Doesn't Matter', 'Thoroughfare Gap', '50 / 50'. Nash solo: 'Military Madness', 'I Used to Be a King', 'Simple Man' (remix), 'Chicago / We Can Change the World', 'Prison Song', 'Another Sleep Song', 'Barrel of Pain (Half-Life)', 'Wild Tales' (1979 live version). Crosby & Nash: 'Song with No Words (Tree with No Leaves)' (Crosby & Nash 1969 version), 'Urge for Going' (intended as 1971 Crosby & Nash single), 'Southbound Train', 'Immigration Man', 'Where Will

I Be?', 'Page 43', 'Carry Me', 'Cowboy of Dreams', 'Bittersweet', 'To the Last Whale...'.

It's rumoured that 'Sea Of Madness' (1969), 'Pushed It Over The End' (1974) and 'Human Highway' (1976) are the three tracks that Nash asked Neil to use on this set, and that Neil agreed, but his manager Elliot Roberts subsequently revoked permission.

'I had a fabulous time doing the box set,' Nash says loftily. 'Because of the longevity of our careers, as a group, in various combinations and solo, I'd forgotten about how much fun we had, how much music we'd made and what kind of an impact we had and continue to have.'

Carry On, a two-disc version for the European and Australian markets drops most of the solo/duo songs: 'Woodstock' (unreleased mix), 'Marrakesh Express', 'You Don't Have to Cry' (unreleased version), 'Teach Your Children', 'Love the One You're With', 'Almost Cut My Hair' (unreleased version). 'Wooden Ships', 'Dark Star', 'Helpless', 'Chicago / We Can Change the World', 'Cathedral', '4+20' (remix), 'Our House', 'To the Last Whale...', 'Change Partners', 'Just a Song Before I Go', 'Ohio', 'Wasted on the Way', 'Southern Cross', 'Suite: Judy Blue Eyes', 'Carry On / Questions', 'Horses Through a Rainstorm' (previously unreleased song), 'Johnny's Garden', 'Guinnevere' (unreleased version), 'Helplessly Hoping' (unreleased version), 'The Lee Shore' (unreleased version), 'Taken At All' (unreleased version), 'Shadow Captain', 'As I Come of Age' (unreleased version), 'Drive My Car' (unreleased version), 'Dear Mr. Fantasy' (previously unreleased song), 'In My Dreams', 'Yours and Mine', 'Haven't We Lost Enough?', 'After the Dolphin', 'Find the Cost of Freedom'.

The Acoustic Concert

Released: 15 March 2005 (US). Highest chart position: 24 (US), 38 (UK).

CSN(Y) included acoustic sets in their live tours from the very start. After a short wholly acoustic series of shows in January 1987, their first full-length acoustic tour took place in 1989, followed by several more in 1990, 1991, 1992 and 1994.

They filmed an excellent segment for *MTV Unplugged* in September 1990.

The video *The Acoustic Concert* was recorded at San Francisco's Warfield Theatre on 10 November 1991. It was re-released on DVD in 2004. The setlist is typical of CSN concerts at the time: 'Déjà Vu', 'Helplessly Hoping', 'Just A Song Before I Go', 'Guinevere', 'Marrakesh Express', 'Long Time Gone', 'To the Last Whale...', 'Try to Find Me' (Nash solo), 'A Thousand Roads' (Crosby solo), 'For What It's Worth' (Stills solo), 'Taken at All', 'Wooden Ships' and 'Suite: Judy Blue Eyes' with encores of 'Our House', 'Daylight Again / Find the Cost of Freedom' and 'Teach Your Children'.

CSN were really on top form during this period, so enjoy some of their best songs in this stripped down and engaging concert DVD.

Greatest Hits

Released: 15 March 2005 (US). Highest chart position: 24 (US), 38 (UK).

Graham Nash dug deep into the band's archives in the ten years from 2005 to 2014. In addition to a new greatest hits package (2005), he co-produced three expansive box sets– *Voyage* (2006), *Reflections* (2009) and *Carry On* (2013)– and an extensive audio document of CNSY's 1974 tour. He has also expressed his wish to remix *Déjà Vu* and issue the unheard 1993 Crosby & Nash album.

Greatest Hits is a hits collection which returned CSN to the top 40 in the US and the UK. It includes all of CSN's hit singles but misses both 'Woodstock' and 'Ohio', which both feature Neil Young. Indeed, Young does not appear on any of the tracks on this album. 'See the Changes' is from the *Stills* album (1975), recorded with Crosby and Nash in 1970.

Tracklist: 'Suite: Judy Blue Eyes', 'Long Time Gone', 'Just a Song Before I Go', 'Southern Cross', 'Marrakesh Express', 'Helplessly Hoping', 'Shadow Captain', 'Our House', 'Guinnevere', 'See the Changes', 'Teach Your Children', 'Wooden Ships', 'Delta', '49 Bye-Byes', 'Wasted on the Way', 'Carry On / Questions', 'In My Dreams', 'Cathedral', 'Daylight Again'.

We should also mention a promo CD given away with copies of the *Daily Mail* in 2005. This includes 1982 live versions of 'Love the One You're With', 'Wooden Ships', 'Long Time Gone', 'Teach Your Children', 'Suite: Judy Blue Eyes', 'For What It's Worth' and 'Wasted on the Way', all taken from the *Daylight Again* DVD (the last two are on *Allies* as well), and 1991 live takes of 'Marrakesh Express' and 'Guinnevere' from *The Acoustic Concert*. 'Lay Me Down' from *Crosby*Nash* and 'Drivin' Thunder' from *Man Alive!* are also included, as well as four tracks from *Man Alive!* playable only on your computer's CD drive. How quaint.

Voyage, Reflections, Carry On

Released: 21 November 2006, 3 February 2009, 2 February 2013.

This series of box sets focus on the individual and solo work of Crosby, Nash and Stills respectively. *Voyage* has sixteen unreleased songs/mixes; Reflections has 33; *Carry On* 28. Several of these are from CSN / CSNY projects and these are all discussed in the main body of the text.

Demos

Released: 2 June 2009 (US). Highest chart position 104 (US), did not chart in the UK.

A mixed bag of demos recorded between 1968 and 1971. Nine of these were previously unreleased. Nash:

> There are 48 demos of our most famous songs that we found in the process of listening to [a] mountain of tapes. I know it's silly, but I think that people are

kind of interested to see that initial spark, that strike of lightning when you put something down on tape at three in the morning and you're a little drunk or something. To compare those to the records that were made from those songs is an interesting transition.

CSN demo: 'Marrakesh Express' – a sprightly and very charming demo from late 1968, just acoustic guitar and vocals. Stills is either absent or inaudible.

Crosby demos: 'Almost Cut My Hair', 'Déjà Vu'. Two remarkable recordings from 1969. 'Almost Cut My Hair', with Crosby on 12-string, is menacing. This had been first released three years earlier on *Voyage*. 'Déjà Vu' is the complete arrangement with an extraordinary scat section: jazz from another planet. This is very different from the Crosby & Nash demo previously released on *Voyage*.

Crosby, Nash, and Young demo: 'Music Is Love'. The basic track of the recording released on Crosby's debut album.

Crosby and Stills demo: 'Long Time Gone'. One of the three songs that made up the 'Frozen Noses' demo tape recorded mid-1968. After circulating for years in collectors' circles, this recording was first officially released in 2006 on *Voyage*.

Stills demos: 'You Don't Have to Cry', 'My Love Is a Gentle Thing', 'Singing Call', 'Love the One You're With'. 'You Don't Have to Cry' is a shortened version of the song from *Crosby, Stills & Nash*. 'My Love Is a Gentle Thing' is a 1968 slow version of the same song released on the CSN box set. 'Singing Call' is the same 1970 demo used on *Stills Alone* but without the excessive reverb. It's very good, indeed. 'Love the One You're With' from April 1970 is wholly acoustic and seemingly off the cuff.

Nash demos: 'Sleep Song', 'Be Yourself', 'Chicago'. Three demos from songs that would be released on Nash's debut solo album, *Songs for Beginners*. The first two named are just Nash and his acoustic guitar, he plays piano on the third.

CSN 2012

This is the most recent and presumably last new album from Crosby, Stills and Nash, recorded during the first leg of their year-long 2012 world tour and released on 2 July 2012. The recordings are rough and ready with those famous harmonies just about intact, with vocal help from James Raymond (keyboards, vocals), Shayne Fontayne (guitar, vocals) and Todd Caldwell (organ, vocals). The rhythm section comprises Kevin McCormick (bass) and Steve DiStanislao (drums). There are seemingly no overdubs or patch-ups, so it's variable in quality: 'Cathedral' is very good indeed but parts of 'Carry On' and 'Southern Cross' are painful. It's probably best enjoyed as a DVD.

CSN 2012 includes three new songs:

'Almost Gone (The Ballad of Bradley Manning)' (Nash / Raymond)

A human-rights song from Graham Nash and James Raymond, first performed during the Crosby-Nash tour of 2011. The song 'acknowledging Manning's role in making public videos and documents that shed light on such as issues as the true number and cause of civilian casualties in Iraq, human rights abuses by U.S.-funded contractors and foreign militaries, and the role that spying and bribes play in international diplomacy.' Nash and Raymond released a studio version in 2011. Its sound and message echo 'Barrel of Pain' from 1980.

'Radio' (Crosby)

A highlight of the album – another of Crosby's excellent late-period songs with an effortlessly commercial chorus ('Look out / Look down / Reach your hand into the water / Pull someone out of the sea'). Crosby returns to his familiar metaphor of a sea journey as a voyage through life – a compilation of all of Crosby's marine-related songs would be excellent: 'Wooden Ships', 'The Lee Shore', 'Shadow Captain', 'Delta', 'Compass', 'Radio'.

David Crosby: 'the idea [of 'Radio'] is that you can actually make a difference in other people's lives and, and you know, it's a question of whether you want to bother and I think people should. I certainly do.'

Crosby would record 'Radio' for his 2014 solo album *Croz*.

'Girl from the North Country' (Dylan)

A favourite of Stills', first released by Dylan in 1962. This arrangement is acoustic, like Dylan's, but with three voices. Another CSN live version (from The Beacon, New York, October 2012) is included on the *Carry On* box set. Stills would re-record 'Girl from the North Country' for his 2017 duo album with old flame Judy Collins.

CSN 2012 also includes live versions of 'Marrakesh Express', 'Long Time Gone', 'Wooden Ships', 'Helplessly Hoping', 'Guinnevere' and 'Suite: Judy Blue Eyes' from *Crosby Stills & Nash;* 'Carry On / Questions', 'Déjà Vu', 'Our House' and 'Teach Your Children' from *Déjà Vu*; 'Cathedral' from *CSN*; and 'Southern Cross' and 'Wasted on the Way' from *Daylight Again*. From Stills solo albums are versions of 'Love the One You're With' from *Stephen Stills*; 'Johnny's Garden' and 'So Begins the Task' from *Manassas*; 'As I Come of Age' from *Stills*. From Nash solo albums: 'Military Madness' from *Songs for Beginners*; and 'In Your Name' from *Reflections*. From Crosby / Nash albums: 'Lay Me Down' from *Crosby*Nash*. And two songs by Buffalo Springfield: 'Bluebird' and 'For What It's Worth'.

We'll also include here the 2011 DVD / Blu-ray release *A Musicares Tribute to Neil Young*, a gala concert held in Los Angeles on 29 January 2010 at which Young declined to appear. CSN sing 'Human Highway', wonderfully. One guitar, three voices in perfect harmony. For three minutes we're back at Wally Heider's in 1969.

CSNY 1974

CSNY's two-month 'Doom Tour' between July and September 1974 was a lucrative 35-date tour, with most of the concerts held in outdoor stadia to many thousands of fans. It was the largest tour so far by any rock band, excessive and extravagant. On the tour Crosby, Stills, Nash and Young were backed by Tim Drummond, the bassist for Young's Stray Gators band, drummer Russ Kunkel from Stills' live band, and percussionist Joe Lala, a member of Manassas.

This three CD set presents an idealised concert from ten different shows Each concert would last three hours or more, with material taken from both group and solo projects. Producers Graham Nash and Joel Bernstein selected the best take for each song from the dozen or so performances available. Sometimes multiple takes or fixes such as tuning and / or flying in parts from other performances would be needed. In the end, forty songs would be released from concerts recorded on 14, 15, 19, 20, 21, 27, 28, 29 August 1974; 14 September 1974; and 14 December 1974. The release date was 8 July 2014 (US) and it charted well in both the US (no. 17) and the UK (no. 37). Nostalgia ain't what it used to be.

The results are mixed. Stills' singing and playing are variable at best in the opening electric sequence. Crosby and Nash sound hoarse and tired, especially during the third set. But when the band were on-form– a stately 'Ohio', a gorgeous 'Carry Me', a tight 'Don't Be Denied', an enervating 'Grave Concern', a definitive 'On the Beach', a soaring 'Carry On', a furious 'Wooden Ships', a glorious 'Helpless', an astounding 'Old Man' – you can understand what the fuss was about. David Crosby:

> Joel and Graham really spent probably over three years pulling that together. And they were very thorough. I think it's a very complete, very, very good choices made, you know, [a] document of that time. The thing that I like the best, and, and they caught it, was that we were very adventuresome. We were very, very willing to take chances. We would do a brand new song and people would join in on it the first time they heard it. Stuff would happen that was obviously unscripted, you know, and, and that was the norm rather than, than the exception and that attitude get captured on the record, you know. And I think that's one of the best things that there was about CSNY. I think that's why Neil liked the band, was that it would be on edge and out in unpredictable territory, most of the time. And it's certainly one of the main reasons I liked it, you know.

From *Crosby Stills & Nash*, there are new recordings of 'Wooden Ships', 'Guinnevere' (from a Crosby/Nash concert in December 1974), 'Suite: Judy Blue Eyes', 'Pre-Road Downs' and 'Long Time Gone'. The in-concert arrangement of Lennon and McCartney's 'Blackbird' is also included. From *Déjà Vu* they perform 'Helpless', 'Almost Cut My Hair', 'Our House', 'Teach Your Children' and 'Déjà Vu'. 'The Lee Shore' was first released on *4 Way Street*. The 1970 single a-side 'Ohio' was usually the first song of the final encore.

For a band with only group two albums to their name, their lengthy sets inevitably included lots of solo material. From Crosby-Nash albums: 'Immigration Man' from *Graham Nash David Crosby*; 'Carry Me' and 'Fieldworker' from the forthcoming *Wind on the Water*; 'Time After Time' from the forthcoming *Whistling Down the Wire*. From Stills' solo albums: horrible electric versions of 'Love the One You're With' and 'Black Queen' from *Stephen Stills*; 'Change Partners' and 'Word Game' from *Stephen Stills 2*; 'Johnny's Garden' from *Manassas*; and 'Myth of Sisyphus' and 'My Angel' from the forthcoming *Stills*. From Nash's solo albums: 'Military Madness' and 'Chicago' from *Songs for Beginners*; 'Grave Concern' and 'Prison Song' from *Wild Tales*. From Young's solo albums: 'Only Love Can Break Your Heart' from *After the Gold Rush*; 'Old Man' from *Harvest*; 'Don't Be Denied' from *Time Fades Away*; 'On the Beach' and 'Revolution Blues' from *On the Beach*; 'Mellow My Mind' from the forthcoming *Tonight's the Night*; 'Long May You Run' from the forthcoming *Long May You Run* and four unreleased songs: 'Traces', 'Goodbye Dick', 'Love Art Blues' and 'Hawaiian Sunrise'.

And then we have 'Pushed It Over the End'. David Crosby: 'One of the most intense pieces of music I've ever heard in my life. It might be the single best Neil Young song.'

16 May 1974. The Bottom Line, New York City. Neil Young plays an unannounced hour-long solo set of mostly new songs: debut live performances of 'Long May You Run', 'On the Beach', 'Motion Pictures' and 'Pardon My Heart' and the unreleased songs 'Ambulance Blues', 'Revolution Blues', 'Roll Another Number (For the Road)' and 'Dance, Dance, Dance'. His set opened with an incredible, dense, powerful track called 'Citizen Kane Junior Blues'. 'Good lookin' Milly's into politics now,' he sang, 'And things are looking much better. She keeps ten men in her garage, knitting her fine sweaters.' Less than two months later, renamed 'Pushed It Over the End', this awesome song was a dark highlight of the CSNY tour. A live-in-Chicago version was released on an Italian promo on 1981. This has backing vocals spruced up in the studio and was scheduled for the *CSN* box set at one time. An alternative, but nowhere near as good, version of 'Pushed It Over the End' from London is on *CSNY 1974*. This song would have been a career highlight for most songwriters, but Young never performed it again after the CSNY tour.

Other songs known to have performed at least once on the tour include: 'For Free', 'Triad', 'What Are Their Names?' (all sung by Crosby); '4+20', 'So Begins the Task', 'First Things First', 'Helpless Hoping', 'Know You Got to Run', 'My Favourite Changes', 'As I Come of Age' (all Stills songs); Chuck Berry's 'You Can't Catch Me'; Nash's 'It's All Right', 'Simple Man', 'Southbound Train', 'Sleep Song', and 'Another Sleep Song'; and 'Down by the River', 'Cowgirl in the Sand', 'Sugar Mountain', 'Ambulance Blues', 'Walk On', 'Human Highway', 'Heart of Gold', 'Homefires', 'On the Way Home', 'Out on the Weekend', 'Birds', 'For the Turnstiles', 'Mellow My Mind', 'Harvest', 'Star of Bethlehem', 'Pardon My Heart', 'Roll Another Number (For the Road)', 'The Losing End', A Man Needs a Maid', 'The Needle and the Damage Done' and 'The Old

Homestead', all by Young.

Stills' 'Carry On', which closed the band's main set every night on the tour, is a notable absentee from the released album. The filmed version from Wembley that leaked years ago is so awful and lasts so long thanks to a dull and self-indulgent extended guitar jam, that one assumes that Nash was unable to rescue it, or couldn't be bothered. But we should congratulate Graham Nash on his diligence in completing this complex project. Other than a handful of highlights no-one's going to listen to it more than once.

Over the Years

Released: 29 June 2018 (US). Highest chart position 27 (UK), did not chart in the US.

A two-CD Graham Nash retrospective, *Over the Years* (2018), collects fifteen Nash songs from 1969 to 2016 – two-thirds of them date from 1969 to 1972.

Track list: 'Marrakesh Express' (Crosby, Stills & Nash), 'Military Madness' (Graham Nash), 'Immigration Man' (Crosby & Nash), 'Just A Song Before I Go' (Crosby, Stills & Nash), 'I Used to Be a King' (Graham Nash), 'Better Days' (Graham Nash), 'Simple Man'(Graham Nash), 'Teach Your Children' (Crosby, Stills, Nash & Young), 'Lady of the Island' (Crosby, Stills & Nash), 'Wind on the Water' (Crosby & Nash), 'Our House' (Crosby, Stills, Nash & Young), 'Cathedral' (Crosby, Stills & Nash), 'Wasted On The Way' (Crosby, Stills & Nash), 'Chicago / We Can Change The World' (Graham Nash), 'Myself at Last' (Graham Nash)

A second disc has with fifteen demos, most of which were unreleased at this point, and all of which are very good. For CSN(Y) collectors, we have previously unheard demos of 'Pre-Road Downs' and 'Teach Your Children' (both February 1969), 'Our House' (November 1969), 'Just a Song Before I Go' (November 1976) and 'Wasted on the Way' (October 1980, with Stephen Stills and Timothy B Schmidt) as well as demos of 'Sleep Song', 'Man in the Mirror', Wind on the Water' and two unheard Nash songs from January 1972.

Transmission Impossible

2018 also saw the release of *Transmission Impossible*, one of a series of semi-legal box sets of radio broadcasts from the likes of David Bowie, Emmylou Harris, Fleetwood Mac, Cream, Eagles, AC / DC and many others.

The CSNY box includes the acoustic set from the Fillmore East in New York, 4 June 1970, sixteen songs from the Roosevelt Raceway on Long Island, 8 September 1974, and the FM broadcast of the Bill Graham Memorial Concert, held in Golden Gate Park in San Francisco, 3 November 1991. The 1970 set is essential for 'Suite: Judy Blue Eyes', 'Guinnevere' and 'Simple Man', the only place you can officially hear renditions of these songs from the 1970 concerts.

Disc 1 (Fillmore East in New York, 4 June 1970)
'Suite: Judy Blue Eyes', 'On the Way Home', 'Teach Your Children', 'Tell Me Why', 'Triad', 'Guinnevere', 'Simple Man', 'Man in the Mirror', 'Cinnamon Girl', 'Down by the River', 'Only Love Can Break Your Heart', 'Black Queen', '49 Bye-Byes / America's Children', 'Love the One You're With'.

Disc 2 (Roosevelt Raceway, Westbury, NY, 8 September 1974)
'Love the One You're With', 'Wooden Ships', 'Immigration Man', 'Helpless', 'Military Madness', 'Johnny's Garden', 'Walk On', 'Almost Cut My Hair', 'Teach Your Children', 'Only Love Can Break Your Heart', 'The Lee Shore', 'Time After Time', 'Southbound Train', 'Another Sleep Song', 'Our House', 'Hawaiian Sunrise'.

Disc 3 (Bill Graham Memorial, Golden Gate Park, San Francisco, CA, 3 November 1991) 'Teach Your Children', 'Love the One You're With', 'Long May You Run', 'Long Time Gone', 'Southern Cross', 'Only Love Can Break Your Heart', 'Wooden Ships', 'Ohio'.

Unreleased And Incomplete Albums

CSNY was always a loose aggregate, coming together when the muse struck them. Many group projects fell apart: there are more unreleased albums in the CSN(Y) timeline than you might imagine.

In 1973-1976, multiple attempts were made to record the second CSNY album. A 1978 follow-up to *CSN* was likewise left incomplete. A projected 1985 album to have been called *As I Come of Age* was abandoned and several more tracks from sessions in 1987 have never been heard after the project morphed into a CSNY album. History repeated ten years later when an entire CSN album of new material from 1997-1998 was shelved once Neil Young came on board for *Looking Forward*. Finally, a long-planned album of cover versions was started with producer Rick Rubin in 2010.

May – June 1973 sessions

> What brought us together in 1973 came out of a giant fog of psychic and musical connections between the four of us, some unspoken, some spoken.
> Graham Nash, quoted in *Crosby, Stills and Nash: The Biography.*

Crosby, Stills, Nash and Young holidayed together in Lahaina on the island of Maui in Hawaii in late Spring 1973. Reconciled, at least temporarily, recording sessions took place for a projected new album at Young's Broken Arrow ranch in Redwood City during May and June 1973, utilising bassist Tim Drummond and drummer Johnny Barbata. The album was to be called *Human Highway* but was never completed, despite further sessions between December 1974 and January 1975, and yet more in April 1976. A few tracks from these sessions have been made available officially: it's unclear how many of those that remain unheard are complete or even still exist.

'See the Changes' (Stills)

A lovely Stephen Stills song, recorded 28 June 1973. This mostly acoustic version is available on the *CSN* box set (1991). For the first time, Neil Young sings on a non-Young CSNY song, adding a winning fragility to the vocal blend. The song was later re-recorded in January 1977 for the *CSN* album.

'Through My Sails' (Young)

An exquisite Neil Young song, recorded by CSNY in 1973 and released on *Zuma* in November 1975: acoustic guitar, bass, sparse percussion and those four voices. Imagine four men, on the beach in Hawaii, happy in each other's company. Perfection.

'Prison Song' (Nash)

The circulating outtake is the same performance as the released version from

Nash's *Wild Tales*, recorded Summer 1973 but with some mix differences. The electric piano, drums, bass, harmonica and lead vocals are identical in both versions. The CNSY version was broadcast on the radio some years ago and has Stills' and Young's backing vocals and electric guitars – Young lays down some shimmery vibrato guitar lines. Nash's released solo mix replaces these with David Lindley's mandolin.

'And So It Goes' (Nash)

Unreleased CSNY song, recorded at Young's ranch and performed by CSNY at their 55-minute October 1973 Winterland reunion concert. Nash would later record the song for his *Wild Tales* album, with Neil Young on piano, David Crosby on backing vocals, Johnny Barbata on drums and Tim Drummond on bass. It sounds so much like a Neil Young song that Nash had to defend himself by claiming that the chord change from Em to F is used by everyone.

'As I Come of Age' (Stills)

The 2013 box set *Carry On* includes a 1973 mix of 'As I Come of Age', a Crosby, Stills and Nash song recorded for Stills' first solo album in 1970 (Ringo on drums!) but not released until the *Stills* album in 1975. It's possible that this, too, was part of the *Human Highway* project: it was performed at the band's Winterland reunion in October 1973. The song was attempted again in 1978, 1981 and 1984-1985. There is also a TV performance from 1991. You should listen to the Pointer Sisters' terrific cover version as well.

'Little Blind Fish' (Crosby)

An unreleased CSNY song, recorded in Spring 1974 during rehearsals for the Doom Tour and later broadcast on KROQ in Los Angeles. CSNY trade vocals over some punchy Stills-Young guitar interplay. Nash noted:

> David wrote some changes and the 'little blind fish' part. Neil wrote the next part. Then I wrote a part that goes 'Hold on, hold on, hold on, I'm coming'. Stephen wrote the last part. And this is the only song that CSNY all had a hand in writing.

It was eventually re-recorded for the first CPR album, with Crosby's lyrical contribution set to music by Jeff Pevar.

December 1974 – January 1975 sessions

'I love singing with those guys,' Neil Young said in 1975, 'but CSNY tends to get too big. Too many people attach too much importance to them. I enjoy being able to visit, but I want to avoid people thinking, 'Oh, there's Neil Young from CSNY.'

'We went down to the Record Plant in Sausalito, rented some studio time'

Young told Cameron Crowe in 1975, 'and left with two things in the can, a song of David's ['Homeward Through the Haze'] and a song of Graham's ['Wind on the Water'] that were great. We really did accomplish some things at those sessions. And just because the sessions only lasted three days, people started building up bullshit stories.'

Further sessions were planned early in 1975, but Neil didn't attend.

'Homeward Through the Haze' (Crosby)

Crosby in one of his darker moods: 'First rain of winter / First fall from grace / It's my first hollow echo / In the halls of praise'. Recorded on 16 December 1974, this is a smoky song that gradually coalesces into something magnificent. This CSNY version was first released on the *CSN* box set, and there is an alternative mix on the *Voyage* box set. The song was re-recorded by Crosby and Nash in June 1975 for their second duo album, *Wind on the Water*.

'We'd gotten together to do a CSNY album,' Crosby recalls, 'but this was the only song that got cut. We had an argument that night, everybody went home and never came back. It was a finding-your-way song at a time when it was getting more and more difficult to find the way. I originally wrote 'Homeward Through the Haze' on guitar and then figured out how to do it on the piano, which I liked a lot better.'

'Wind on the Water' (Nash)

Unreleased CSNY version of song that later formed part of 'To the Last Whale…' from Crosby & Nash's 1975 album *Wind on the Water*. The master tapes were supposedly destroyed by Stephen Stills, but we may never know.

'Carry Me' (Crosby), **'Time After Time'** (Crosby)

Two David Crosby songs from December 1974, later recorded for Crosby & Nash's 1975 album *Wind on the Water*. They are both terrific songs: 'Carry Me' is, unusually for Crosby, self-reflective, and 'Time After Time' has a tender melody that simply aches. One assumes that the CSNY versions were left incomplete.

'Different Tongues' (Stills / Dacus)

Later recorded in March 1976 for *Illegal Stills*.

'Western Witches' (Stills?)

An unknown song, possibly written by Stephen Stills, recorded January 1975.

'Guardian Angel' (Stills)

The last song from the January 1975 sessions, recorded after Young had left. Stills and Nash had an argument over a harmony line on this song and this ended the sessions. It was later revisited for *Long May You Run*.

1976 sessions

Graham Nash:

> One day in [April] 1976 Neil came by my house in San Francisco. He played us a tape of some sessions he and Stephen had been recording at Criteria Studios in Miami: 'Black Coral', 'Midnight on the Bay', 'Human Highway'. It sounded great, but then Neil said, 'Isn't there something missing?' And Crosby goes, 'Yeah, us,' meaning me and David. So the next morning we were on a plane to Miami. We added harmonies to their existing tracks, and recorded some new songs, 'Taken at All' being one of them. But David and I had to return to Los Angeles to finish our album, and Stephen and Neil had to wrap theirs up so they'd have product to push with the Stills / Young Band tour. The Crosby-Nash harmonies were transferred to safeties, then wiped from the master tapes.

Crosby was livid at the time. 'I have nothing but contempt for those two,' he said then. 'I refuse to be on call for them any longer.'

Three songs have been officially released; another has been broadcast on the radio.

'Taken at All' (Nash / Crosby)

A highlight of the *CSN* box set. A highlight of their entire recorded body. The author's favourite CSNY song: four guitars, four voices, one take. 'Personally, this is my favourite CSNY track,' recalls Graham Nash. 'Written about the group situation in 1976: Can this road be taken at all?'

It's clear from this song that Nash was hurt more than anyone else about CSNY's failure to get it together again in 1973, 1974 and 1975 – 'Is this road really the only way? / Can this road be taken, taken at all? / We lost it on the highway / Down the dotted line / You were going your way / I was going mine'.

Crosby and Nash had already recorded their own more sluggish arrangement two weeks prior to these sessions and this can be heard on *Whistling Down the Wire*. A remix on *Reflections* sounds exactly the same to me.

'Human Highway' (Young)

CSNY's version of this Neil Young song is in circulation after engineer Stephen Barncard played it on a radio show called 'Dead to the World' on KPFK in San Francisco in 1996. It's a pensive acoustic take, probably from the same sessions as 'Taken at All'. Young would re-record in 1978. The CSNY version has Stills on dobro. At one time in contention for the *CSN* box set, perhaps it will be released on Young's second volume of *Archives*?

'Black Coral' (Stills), 'Long May You Run' (Young)

Dating from April 1976, these are two tracks originally recorded for the Stills-Young Band album. Crosby and Nash's backing vocals were added but later removed after the inevitable falling out.

The CSNY mix of 'Black Coral' can be heard on Stephen Stills' *Carry On* box set. It's quite brilliant.

'Long May You Run' might be an ode to Young's car, but could easily be about Crosby, Stills, Nash and Young – 'We've been through some things together / With trunks of memories still to come.' The song had been performed by Stills and Young during CSNY's acoustic sets on their 1974 tour and was an obvious choice for the lead track on the 1976 Still-Young Band project: Young had chosen not to record the song for *Zuma*. The full band 'Long May You Run' is on Neil Young's 1976 compilation album *Decade*.

'Midnight on the Bay' (Young), **'Ocean Girl'** (Young)

Two Stills-Young Band songs for which Crosby and Nash added harmonies in April 1976. These were wiped for *Long May You Run*, but the CSNY versions must exist somewhere. Surely?

'Dancer' (Crosby)

Supposedly cut by CSNY in 1976 – if so this version is unreleased. It was subsequently recorded by Crosby and Nash for their *Whistling Down the Wire* duo album in April-May 1976. 'Dancer' is a wordless Crosby tune, not so far from 'Song with No Words (Tree with no Leaves)'. It would sound of our place on a CSNY album, I suspect.

Some sources log Nash's 'Mutiny' as being part of these sessions. Nash wrote later:

> We only had a few days left in Miami, but things were heading perilously downhill. One morning, I couldn't get any reply from Neil's room. I called the front desk of the Mutiny and said, 'Am I out of it? Am I dialling the wrong number?' The receptionist said, 'Oh, no – Mr. Young has checked out.' Whaaaaat? 'Yes, Mr. Young checked out earlier this morning.' 'Going where?' I asked. 'Back to San Francisco.' We were supposed to be in the studio in four hours. Man, some things never change. It was another case of Neil having had enough – whatever enough was supposed to be– and he'd split without telling anyone. I went straight back to my room and began writing 'Mutiny'.
>
> With the ice man cooling the wind / The coastline can't be very far / With the shore man rowing behind / We'll find our way beneath the stars / But the captain sat there and grinned / And he set the sail for Shangri-La. Mutiny at Sail Boat Bay.

I guess we can compile our own album from these 1973-1976 sessions. How about 'See the Changes', 'Taken at All', 'Human Highway' (outtake version), 'Homeward Through the Haze', 'Prison Song' (outtake version), 'As I Come of Age', 'Long May You Run', 'Black Coral' and 'Through My Sails'…?

1978 sessions

CSN released a new, highly successful, album in 1977 and toured the US. They started recording their third trio album in early 1978 at Criteria in Miami, with co-producers Ron and Howard Albert. These sessions were abandoned after a few weeks and none of the songs known to have been attempted have been released. The project was re-assigned as a possible Crosby & Nash album, but Crosby's well-documented drug problems took him out of the picture.

These were the songs logged during six weeks of sessions.

'Distances' (Crosby)

Released on Crosby's *Oh Yes I Can* in 1989. Nash on piano. The 1978 version should have been included on the *Voyage* box set but inexplicably wasn't.

'Drive My Car' (Crosby)

Recorded at Sound Labs in Los Angeles in 1978 and released on the *CSN* box set. Re-recorded for *Oh Yes I Can* in 1986.

'(Got to Keep) Open' (Stills / Nash)

Recorded for Crosby, Stills and Nash's *Live It Up* in 1990.

'Love Has Come' (Nash), **'Helicopter Song'** (Nash)

(Re-)recorded in 1978-1979 for Nash's *Earth & Sky* album. Both songs have Crosby on backing vocals. 'Helicopter Song' has Stills on guitar, too, so probably originates in the CSN sessions.

'That's the Way It Was' (Stills), **'Hold on Tight'** (Stills), **'What's the Game'** (Stills)

Three unreleased Stephen Stills songs. In addition, 'As I Come of Age' (Stills), 'Mirage' (Nash), 'Jigsaw' (Crosby / Nash), 'Down Behind the Waves' (Nash) and 'Paper Glider' (Crosby) are listed as forming part of these sessions– they had all been attempted during sessions for *CSN*, so it could be that these recordings are from 1977, not 1978.

1985: As I Come of Age

A new Crosby, Stills and Nash album, to have been called *As I Come of Age*, was planned for a 1985 release. It would have been taken from many sessions over several years.

Stills said in May 1985:

> We just did the, we call it the 'corporate album','. 'You see, our contract was about to come up, and David went on a ... vacation recently. Needless to say, we couldn't cut very much, so we had to do something real quick 'cuz the record company was real pissed. Contrary to popular belief, this is a business.

So we threw something together. I haven't stayed up for 48 hours in about five years. So, that was hard.

'Lonely Man' (Nash)

Recorded in 1984 (basic track) and 1985 (CSN vocals and Stills' guitar), and performed live a few times, CSN's studio version was released on Nash's *Reflections* box set. With its pattering drum machine and air of incompletion, there's an air of desperation here– it's not Nash's best work and is killed by the cold, digital mid-'80s production that sank *Innocent Eyes*.

'Drive My Car' (Crosby)

Possibly the 1978 version released on the *CSN* box set in 1991.

'Clear Blue Skies' (Nash)

Re-recorded by CSNY for *American Dream*.

'As I Come of Age'

Stills & Nash's 1980 recording

'Melody' (Crosby)

From Crosby's unreleased 1980 solo album.

'You Might Be Loved' (Stills)

A left-over from the *Daylight Again* sessions, with another version recorded late 1988.

'Feed the People' (Stills)

Recorded by CSN in 1985, or perhaps it's an earlier 1979 version from Stills' rejected *Southern Cross* album. Or perhaps it's the 1979 version with later CSN overdubs. Stills would sing this on both CSN's 2001 tour and CSNY's 2002 tour (announced as 'a brand new song'). A studio version is on *Man Alive!* (2005): the presence of singer Brooks Hunnicutt dates some or all of it to 1979, so it could be the CSN version. Or not.

'Distances' (Crosby)

From Crosby's unreleased 1980 solo album. Nash on piano. It dates to CSN sessions in 1978 and was ultimately released on Crosby's *Oh Yes I Can* in 1989.

'Dear Mr. Fantasy' (Winwood / Capaldi / Wood)

Stills & Nash's 1980 recording, released on the *CSN* box set in 1991.

1987 album sessions

American Dream started as a CSN project with initial sessions in March-April 1987. Songs known to have been recorded but unreleased are 'He's an

American' (Crosby), 'Lover' (Stills) and 'Water from the Moon' (Nash).There is a version of the last-named on the *Reflections* box set where is credited as a solo song but sounds a lot like Crosby, Stills and Nash.

1996-1999 album sessions

Crosby, Stills and Nash terminated their contract with Atlantic in 1997. Nash to Debbie Kruger in 1999:

> The relationship with Atlantic Records was always a personal one. Our friend and mentor, Ahmet Ertegun, was our main contact at Atlantic and our relationship was based on mutual respect. He is a fine musician, singer and producer. However, during the last few years as Ahmet got older, he had less and less to do with the daily running of the company. After the lukewarm promotion of our last couple of records, we felt nobody at the company really understood us and cared about us. They seemed to be following the usual game of 'throwing' stuff at the wall and seeing what sticks. In days past, record companies were committed to working a band over several singles not just giving up if the first single did not set the charts on fire. We felt abandoned and we left Atlantic Records after almost 30 years with them.

Crosby, Stills and Nash began to record new tracks out of their own pockets, without a record deal. Initial sessions took place at Ga Ga's Room in Los Angeles between November 1996 and January 1997. Overdubs in April 1998 at Ocean Way Studios, Burbank, resulted in a completed album. A tentative December 1998 tracklist included 'No Tears Left', 'Half Your Angels', 'Morrison', 'Acadienne', 'Heartland', 'Mystery', 'Lost Another One', 'Isn't It So', 'Everybody's Talkin'' (a 1969 version with new overdubs) and 'Faith in Me'.

'Half Your Angels' (Nash)

Written by Graham Nash after the 1995 Oklahoma City bombings, recorded by CSN in 1998 and performed over 150 times by CSN(Y) between 1995 and 2003. Never released commercially, CSN's version was made available as a free download via the CSN website after the 9/11 attacks in 2001. This hard-to-find version is the last ever studio release credited to 'Crosby, Stills and Nash'. It's one of Nash's best songs, world-weary but with a glimmer of hope: 'Send me half your angels / We're running out of time / Send me half your angels / I'll send you half of mine'. Crosby and Nash re-recorded the song with a more subdued feel on their 2004 album *Crosby Nash*.

'No Tears Left' (Stills)

Retained for, and released on, *Looking Forward*.

'Morrison' (Crosby / Raymond)

Co-written by James Raymond. 'I sent off some lyrics I'd been playing around with,' Crosby recalled. 'And James came back with music that sounded like Steely Dan!' This song was performed in concert by CSN over fifty times in 1997-1999 and was the opening song on the debut album by CPR released in August 1997.

'Acadienne' (Stills)
A bouncy, Cajun song performed by Stills in his solo sets at CSN gigs between 1999 and 2005. 'Acadienne' was released on Stills' album *Man Alive!* (2005). Graham Nash is on the *Man Alive!* version, so this may in fact be the 1996-1997 recording.

'Heartland' (Nash)
Retained for, and released on, *Looking Forward*, with added Young lead guitar.

'Mystery' (Stills)
Recorded in LA in February 1997 but so far unheard. It had previously been attempted during the sessions for *Live it Up*.

'Lost Another One' (Nash)
A touching song about mortality and the death of musician friends, written after the death of Jerry Garcia. Performed since 1995 it was eventually recorded for *Songs for Survivors* (2002), there dedicated to George Harrison.

'Isn't It So' (Stills)
Previously recorded for *Stills Alone*.

'Everybody's Talkin''(Neil)
The 1969 version with new overdubs

'Faith in Me' (Stills)
Retained, and released on for *Looking Forward*, with added Young lead guitar.

Other unreleased songs from the 1996-1997 sessions:

'The Crow on the Cradle' (Carter)
A folk song credited to English poet and songwriter Sydney Carter and a mainstay of the 1960s folk coffee house circuit, where it was sung by everybody from Pete Seeger to Judy Collins to Christie Moore. It originally dates from the sixteenth century. The song was exquisitely sung by Nash with Jackson Browne at the No Nukes concert in 1979 and tried a couple of times in early sessions for *Looking Forward*.

'The Navigator' (Allan Thomas)
Allan Thomas is an American songwriter and musician. 'The Navigator' comes

from his 1997 album *Coconut Culture*. It is a duet with Graham Nash and deploys some distinctive Crosby-style guitar. The CSN version was recorded during sessions for the unreleased album that preceded *Looking Forward* in January 1998.

'Rock and Roll Woman' (Stills)

The Buffalo Springfield song– with Joe Walsh on guitar!

'Turn! Turn! Turn! (To Everything There Is a Season)' (Arr. Pete Seeger)

The title track from The Byrds' second album, performed at CSN concerts of the period.

The Covers Album

The long-mooted but never completed CSN covers album was often discussed by the band on stage: during 2009-2012 they performed many songs by other writers. Studio sessions with Rick Rubin are known to have taken place in 2010-2012, with a handful of songs completed. 'We did seven songs and none of them excited us,' Nash told Billboard in 2014. 'Sony owns those seven songs that they have no right to release them. They have to ask our permission to release them, which we will never give.' An argument between the mercurial producer and the ever-fiery David Crosby derailed the sessions, however.

'If Crosby is not into it – if any of us are not into it,' Nash explained, 'it ends. Evermore so when David doesn't want to do something. We found it very difficult to work with Rick after a while. Rick and Crosby started to get in each other's face and it was over. It was a good idea, but it didn't last.' 'We didn't really successfully generate any masters out of the time when [Rubin] was trying it out with us,' Crosby said, 'I don't think it's his fault. There just wasn't a chemistry.'

Work eventually resumed, without Rubin, at Jackson Browne's Groovemasters studio in 2014. 'We went back to the studio in Santa Monica and started over and we've got five we really like,' Nash said at the time, 'and as soon as get back off the road we're going to go back in and finish it'. But nothing from any of these sessions has so far been released.

Nash has confirmed that 'Behind Blue Eyes' (The Who), 'You Can Close Your Eyes' (James Taylor), 'Norwegian Wood' (The Beatles), 'Across the Universe' (The Beatles) and 'Blackbird' (The Beatles) were planned for the project. Other songs most likely in the frame, based on live performances in this period, include 'Uncle John's Band' (Grateful Dead), 'Reason to Believe' (Tim Hardin), 'Ruby Tuesday' (The Rolling Stones), and 'Midnight Rider' (Allman Brothers Band). These nine songs, no doubt with a few others, would have made an interesting and worthwhile addition to the band's discography. Like the unfinished *Human Highway*, *As I Come of Age* and untitled 1998 albums, however, this is one more 'what if?' in the long and tangled CSN story.

Solo Albums

In the thirty-four years between 'Mr Tambourine Man' and his 57th birthday, David Crosby released precisely three solo albums. In the twenty-two years since he has put out six, with four of those since 2014. Here is a man who has always had a lot to say. And he's saying more as the years advance.

Crosby's debut solo album, *If I Could Only Remember My Name*, was released in February 1971, three months after *Stephen Stills* and two months before *4 Way Street*. Robert Christgau of *Village Voice*, for one, was not impressed.

> This disgraceful performance inspires the first Consumer Guide Competition. The test: Rename David Crosby (he won't know the difference). The prize: One Byrds LP of your choice (he ought to know the difference). The catch: You have to beat my entries. Which are: Rocky Muzak, Roger Crosby, Vaughan Monroe. D-

But any album that includes 'Orleans', 'Traction in the Rain' and the classic 'Laughing' cannot be dismissed lightly. 'Cowboy Movie' semi-fictionalises the tangled web of relationships between Crosby, Nash, Stills, Young and Rita Coolidge. Years later, the album was listed second on the 'Top 10 Pop Albums of All Time' as published in the Vatican City newspaper *L'Osservatore Romano*. It's the Pope's favourite rock album!

Fast forward eighteen years to *Oh Yes I Can* (1989), an upbeat and hopeful album which combines four songs planned for Crosby's unfinished 1979-1981 Capitol Records solo album, another attempted during aborted 1978 sessions for a follow-up to CSN and some excellent new songs, including Crosby's transcendent 'Tracks in the Dust', and 'In the Wide Ruin' by the same writers as 'Might As Well Have a Good Time' from *Daylight Again*.

The uneven *Thousand Roads* (1993) comprises mostly cover versions and co-writes, but includes the impeccable 'Yvette In English', written with Joni Mitchell and recorded by her on *Turbulent Indigo* (1994). Crosby survived another near-death experience in November 1994: a liver transplant funded by his friend and collaborator Phil Collins.

David Crosby's third-act renaissance started with 1998's *CPR*, a mix of rock, jazz, folk and vocal harmonies that partnered him with his son James Raymond and session guitar maestro Jeff Pevar. These two men inspired Crosby to do some of his very best work. Opening with the magnificent, jazz-tinged 'Morrison' *CPR* is a beautifully written, performed and sung album, with much to enjoy including 'Rusty and Blue', 'Somehow She Knew', 'At the Edge' and 'Time Is The Final Currency' which all approach and sometimes surpass Crosby's best songs of the previous thirty years. A follow-up, *Just Like Gravity* was released in 2001 and is also excellent.

Crosby's most recent solo albums, *Croz* (2014), *Lighthouse* (2016), *Sky Trails* (2017) and *Here If You Listen* (2018) plough the same furrow of melodic, slightly jazzy, sometimes self-centred, carefully crafted songs. The last-named has joint credit to Michael League, Becca Stevens and Michelle Willis and is very good indeed. Also, don't overlook's Crosby's superb collaboration with League's band Snarky Puppy – 'Somebody Home' from 2016.

Crosby has released a handful of live albums. *It's All Coming Back to Me Now...* (1995) is a robust recording from 1993, with some surprises such as 'In My Dreams' and 'Cowboy Movie'. Graham Nash guests on three songs. *King Biscuit Flower Hour* (1996) presents a 1989 concert, with rare (and wonderful) performances of 'Compass' and 'Delta'. The albums *Live at Cuesta College* (1998) and *Live at the Wiltern* (1999) were recorded with CPR and demonstrate both the strength of Crosby's back catalogue and the musicality of his partners. The former is mostly acoustic, recorded as a trio and includes a devastating performance of one of Crosby's late-period masterpieces 'Somehow She Knew'. *Live at the Wiltern* has a five-piece band with guest appearances by Graham Nash, Phil Collins and others. 'Rusty and Blue' is astonishing. Both albums are highly recommended.

The three-CD box set *Voyage* (2006) compiles the best of Crosby's work with The Byrds, CSN, CSNY, Crosby & Nash, CPR and his solo albums through to 2001. Of most interest to CSN(Y) fans would be the original demos of 'Long Time Gone',' Guinnevere', 'Almost Cut My Hair', 'Déjà Vu' and 'Triad'. There is also the session outtake 'Climber' from *Looking Forward* and an unheard live version of 'Dream for Him' from 2002.

Stephen Stills' solo career began in 1970, but earlier recordings are available. The archive album *Just Roll Tape* (2007), recorded in (probably) July or August 1968 and lost for almost forty years, features a late-night session of Stills, his voice and guitar. There are early versions of 'Suite: Judy Blue Eyes' (no final section), 'Helplessly Hoping' (beautiful), and 'Wooden Ships' (just the chorus at this stage). Several songs from his early solo albums and five unheard gems include 'Judy' finally recorded almost fifty years later. This is Stills at the beginning of his peak period.

The *Supersession* album was recorded around the same time. Stills plays guitar on four tracks. The Donovan cover 'Season of the Witch' is perhaps the most successful.

Stephen Stills (1970) was recorded mostly at Island Studios in London in January and June / July 1970, between the two CSNY tours. It features many well-known musicians including Jimi Hendrix, Eric Clapton, Booker T. Jones, Rita Coolidge, David Crosby, Graham Nash, John Sebastian, Cass Elliott, Ringo Starr and the CSNY rhythm section of Calvin 'Fuzzy' Samuel and John Barbata. The songs are strong, too: not just 'Love the One You're With' but 'Do for the Others', 'To a Flame', 'Sit Yourself Down', 'Black Queen' and the majestic 'We Are Not Helpless'. Essential.

Stephen Stills 2 (1971) recorded in the first half of 1971 is less successful– the horn section perhaps is an overdub too far. It's split between self-indulgence and self-pity, but any album with 'Change Partners', 'Singin' Call' and 'Word

Game' is worth a listen.

It's a moot point whether the *Manassas* album (1972) is a group or solo project. Stills' choice of collaborators here was wise: principally former Byrd and Flying Burrito Brother Chris Hillman, but also pianist Paul Harris from Stills' touring band, steel guitarist and former Burrito Al Perkins, and a killer rhythm section of bassist Fuzzy Samuel (*4 Way Street*) and drummer Dallas Taylor (*Déjà Vu*). Most of the songs are Stills originals, fusing Latin, rock, blues, country, folk and bluegrass influences. His voice was at its gritty soulful best on this album. Four sides no filler, great singing, great playing, great songs. There's not a moment here that is less than wonderful – whether it's the extended medley that fills side one, the pure country of side two (including two of Stills' best ever songs, 'Colorado' and the stately 'So Begins the Task'), the folky songs that fill side three including 'It Doesn't Matter' and 'Johnny's Garden', or the rock-'em-out fourth side. This band was amazing in concert as well, as bootlegs of their shows attest. Stills said at the time that it was the best album he'd been involved in. It's difficult to argue with him.

After Manassas' first album and tour, Stills would reunite with Crosby, Nash and Young for the first sessions of the incomplete *Human Highway* album, and Hillman would record an album with the reunited classic line-up of *The Byrds*. Inevitably, Manassas lost momentum after this. *Down the Road* (1973) and the leftovers collection *Pieces* (2009) attest that Stills' mojo departed him around the time of the CSNY 'Doom Tour' in 1974. In terms of new songs it would remain elusive: his solo career since has very occasional moments of lucidity, and his work with CSN(Y) has been patchy at best.

Stills (1975) and *Illegal Stills* (1976) have little to recommend them. 'Myth of Sisyphus' and 'My Angel' from *Stills* were performed on the CSNY 1974 tour and are perhaps the highlights from that album. 'Stateline Blues', the best song on *Illegal Stills*, is an acoustic country blues that Stills can perform in his sleep. After an ill-advised reunion with Neil Young on *Long May You Run* (1976), Stills' solo career took a marked dip with the tired *Thoroughfare Gap* (1978) and the mostly unlistenable *Right by You* (1984). The latter does include a sprightly version of 'No Hiding Place' which has contributions from Graham Nash, Chris Hillman, John Sambataro (Firefall) and Herb Pedersen (Desert Rose Band).

Stills Alone (1991) plays on Stills' strengths as a singer and acoustic guitar player, with covers of songs by Fred Neil, Bob Dylan (a scintillating 'Ballad of Hollis Brown') and the Beatles ('In My Life'), as well as the first official release of 'Treetop Flyer', a song first performed in the mid-1970s. *Stills Alone* also includes the 1971 demo version of 'Singin' Call' from *Stephen Stills 2*.

And then nothing for fourteen years until *Man Alive!* (2005), a very mixed bag of half-hearted new rock songs, older unreleased songs with overdubs, re-recordings and collaborations with Neil Young and Graham Nash. The remarkable eleven-minute 'Spanish Suite' closes the album – dating from 1979, it's a career highlight.

Out of the blue, at almost seventy years of age, Stills formed The Rides with Kenny Wayne Shepherd, Barry Goldberg, Kevin McCormick and Chris Layton. They have recorded two tough, bluesy albums, *Can't Get Enough* (2013) and *Pierced Arrow* (2016), with Stills on fine form vocally and instrumentally. To top that, *Everybody Knows* (2017) is a wonderful collaboration with his former lover Judy Collins. They acknowledge mortality and lost love in re-recordings of 'Questions', 'So Begins the Task', 'Who Knows Where the Time Goes', 'Girl from the North Country' and others, along with the first official version of Stills' 'Judy', written for her in 1968. Delicious.

Stills has released two live albums. *Stephen Stills Live* (1975) was recorded just before the CSNY reunion and is a thrilling document of Stills' spring 1974 tour, including a tough 'Wooden Ships', a couple of dusted-off Buffalo Springfield classics and an excellent solo acoustic set which features the first official release of Stills singing 'Everybody's Talkin''. *Live at Shepherd's Bush* (2009) sees a diminished, much older musician who can still hold a tune and an audience. There a couple of surprises: the acoustic 'Blind Fiddler Medley' and a from-the-vaults 'Isn't It About Time' from *Down the Road*.

The four-CD box set *Carry On* (2013) compiles the best of Stills' various group and solo albums from 1962 to 2002. Of most interest to CSN(Y) fans would be the original 1968 demo of '49 Reasons', an unheard live version of 'Find the Cost of Freedom' from 1970, 'Old Man Trouble' from the 2002 tour, and best of all, the CSNY version of 'Black Coral' from the *Long May You Run* sessions.

Graham Nash has released six solo albums. *Songs for Beginners* (1971) is chock-full of great songs including 'Military Madness', performed by Nash at almost every concert he's given since, the heartfelt 'Better Days', the touchingly direct 'Sleep Song' (rejected by the Hollies), the extraordinarily emotional 'Simple Man' and the simply magnificent 'I Used to Be a King'. There are guest appearances from David Crosby, Jerry Garcia, Phil Lesh, Dave Mason, David Lindley, Rita Coolidge and Neil Young. Young himself collaborated with Nash on the rare one-off Young-Nash single 'War Song' in 1972.

Wild Tales (1974) is 'a tame collection of reshuffled platitudes' suggested *Village Voice*. That's harsh, but *Wild Tales* is certainly more sombre in mood and less inspired than Nash's debut. His next two albums, both with David Crosby, are happier and contain some of his best songs.

Earth & Sky (1980) sees Nash's muse starting to depart with very few memorable moments – even the key song, 'Barrel of Pain' is served better by the live arrangement on CSN's *Allies*. *Innocent Eyes* (1986) is a truly horrible album, practically unlistenable as Nash fails to reinvent himself as an '80s synthesiser pop star. His sometimes reedy tenor is lost amongst the clatter of the drum programming. Those of us who bought this in 1986 are still living with the disappointment. *Songs for Survivors* (2002), however, was a dramatic return to form. Sixteen years after *Innocent Eyes*, Nash plays to his key strength – good songs, performed in the traditional singer-songwriter milieu. The pulsating 'Dirty Little Secret' opens a strong album. Nash's sparse reworking of Richard and Linda Thompson's 'Pavanne' is as good as anything else he's released since 1963.

Nash's terrific song 'Burning for the Buddha', written with James Raymond, was performed over eighty times by CSN between 2013 and 2015. 'When we were protesting the Vietnam war, many years ago,' Nash said in 2013, 'there was one image that was spread around the world: the Tibetan monk that burned himself to death in protest. In the last year, one hundred and twenty-eight Tibetan monks have burned themselves to death because of the conflict between Tibet and China.' It was surprisingly not recorded for Nash's sixth solo album *This Path Tonight* (2016). The album, a combination of self-revelation and self-redefinition, was written and recorded quickly in the wake of Nash's estrangement from David Crosby and his separation from his wife of 38 years. 'I was going through all this emotional chaos in my life and I was writing and writing,' he told *Rolling Stone*. 'I still don't know which side of the street to walk on without pissing people off.' *This Path Tonight* is a very personal collection of lean songs, sometimes confessional, sometimes probing: 'The question haunting me / 'Is my future just my past?''. Remarkable really.

The *Reflections* box set (2009) includes an alternative mix of CSNY's 'Teach Your Children' and a CSN take of 'Clear Blue Skies'. There is an otherwise unheard CSN song called 'Lonely Man' from sessions for the incomplete 1984-1985 album *As I Come of Age*. *Over the Years* (2018) collects fifteen of Nash's self-penned songs from 1969 to 2016, although all but four date from 1972 or before. The CD version includes fifteen demos from 1968 through to 1980.

Graham Nash and David Crosby – the 'quiet heart and social conscience of CSNY' as Alan Pattinson has it – have collaborated on four studio albums since 1972. Their three albums together from the 1970s – *Graham Nash David Crosby* (1972), *Wind on the Water* (1975) and *Whistling Down the Wire* (1976) – are chock full of great songs, including long-term set staples 'Immigration Man' and the wonderful 'To the Last Whale'. There is quality in depth as well: 'Naked in the Rain', 'Time After Time', Bittersweet', 'Homeward Through the Haze', 'Taken at All', 'Southbound Train', 'Fieldworker', 'Page 43', the outstanding 'Carry Me' and 'Time After Time'. This music should not be dismissed. The closing song on *Whistling Down the Wire*, the much overlooked 'Out of the Darkness' is a terrific song, the peak of Crosby and Nash's 1970s work together. After several abandoned attempts to record a new album together their fourth (and we assume final) duo album, the prosaically named *Crosby*Nash* came out in August 2004. It is beautifully produced and includes several lovely songs co-written with either James Raymond or Jeff Pevar, as well as some new Crosby and Nash originals including 'Milky Way Tonight', the excellent 'Don't Dig Here' and the radio hit 'Lay Me Down'.A Nash-led project to collect their various sessions for the likes of James Taylor, Bonnie Raitt, Joni Mitchell, Carole King, Kenny Loggins, John Mayer and Jimmy Webb remains unrealised. *Crosby-Nash Live* (1977) is a contract filler but is the only place to hear Crosby's 'King of the Mountain' (on the CD reissue only). ***Another Stoney Evening*** (1998) showcases a complete acoustic duo show from October 1971 and consists of very, erm, relaxed performances of mostly previously released songs from *Crosby, Stills &Nash*, *Déjà Vu* and their recent solo albums *If I Could Only Remember My Name* and *Songs for Beginners*.

To these we can add: Crosby's 1969 album co-written with Paul S Williams but seemingly never recorded; Stills' unreleased *Stolen Stills* album of outtakes from 1970-1971; Stills' *As I Come of Age* album which was reworked as *Stills* in 1975; Crosby's 1978-1980 solo sessions repurposed for *Daylight Again*; Stills' idea for a Latin album in 1979 from which only two or three songs were completed; the Stephen Stills unreleased album *Southern Cross* from 1980; unfinished sessions for Crosby & Nash albums in 1979, 1989 and 1993.

Neil Young, meanwhile, has ploughed his own furrow for more than fifty years: even a short resume of his lengthy and erratic solo career would take many pages. Let's just say that if you're new to Neil Young's solo work, start with his flawless trio of albums from 1969 to 1972 (*Everybody Knows This Is Nowhere*, *After the Goldrush* and *Harvest*), the 1979 live album *Live Rust* and then back to *Zuma* (1975), *Tonight's the Night* (released 1975, recorded 1973) and *On the Beach* (1974). Add *Freedom* (1989), *Ragged Glory* (1990) and *Harvest Moon* (1992) and you have the ten most essential Young solo albums. Tread carefully after the mid-nineties: there's much to enjoy but also excessive padding and retreads of past glories.

The Future?

As 2020 ends, David Crosby will be 79 years old; Stills, 75; Nash, 78 and Young, 75. They have been nothing if not productive since the mid-1960s: hardly a year has gone by without at least one new album of new songs by one of these four men. As recently as 2016, there were new albums by all four of them – *Lighthouse* (Crosby), *Pierced Arrow* (Stills with the Rides), *This Path Tonight* (Nash) and *Peace Trail* (Young).

But CSN, as an active band, seem to be over. Crosby had called Nash's 2013 memoir *Wild Tales* 'a very shallow, very self-serving book, and full of BS' and Nash responded complaining that driving his partners was 'like pushing a big rock up a hill, and it's slipping back. And I ran out of patience with it all.'

In 2014, Crosby was asked by the *Idaho Statesman* to respond to the news that Neil Young had filed for divorce from his wife of nearly 40 years and was in a relationship with Daryl Hannah. 'I happen to know that he's hanging out with somebody that's a purely poisonous predator now. And that's karma. He's gonna get hurt. But I understand why it happened. I'm just sad about it. I'm always sad when I see love get tossed in the gutter.' Crosby subsequently apologised. 'I was completely out of line,' he told Howard Stern. 'I have screwed up massively. Daryl Hannah never wound up in a Texas prison. I'm screwed up way worse than that girl. Where do I get off criticising her? She's making Neil happy. I love Neil and I want him happy.'

But the damage had been done. CSN's last live appearance together was mangling 'Silent Night' in Washington DC on 3 December 2015. Watch the video on YouTube– Nash would clearly rather be anywhere else. 'This was very sad,' says Nash. 'Stephen and David ended up fighting after it. Stephen then threw a [guitar] pick at David. It was over from that moment. They started fighting backstage and we never spoke again after that. I talk to Stephen and I talk to Neil, but not David.'

'I don't like David Crosby right now,' Nash added in 2016. 'He's been awful for me the last two years, just fucking awful. I've been there and saved his fucking ass for 45 years, and he treated me like shit. You can't do that to me. You can do it for a day or so, until I think you're going to come around. When it goes on longer, and I keep getting nasty emails from him, I'm done. Fuck you. David has ripped the heart out of Crosby, Stills, Nash and Young.'

'I still have friends,' says Crosby in the Grammy-nominated *Remember my Name* documentary, 'but all of the guys I made music with won't even talk to me. One of them hating my guts could be an accident. But McGuinn, Nash, Neil and Stephen all really dislike me, strongly.' Nash:

> I was [Crosby's] best friend for so many years. I saved his ass on so many levels it's insane. For him to treat one of his so-called best friends the way Crosby has treated me, I just won't stand for it, I'm afraid. Right now, I don't want anything to do with Crosby at all. It's just that simple. In my world there will never, ever be a Crosby, Stills, Nash and Young record and there will never be another

Crosby, Stills and Nash record or show. Originally we were all in love with each other. We were in love with the songs. We were in love with the energy. I hardly knew Stephen when we started. Developing those friendships was all very well. But as usual with family, after 50 years, sometimes you don't agree with your family. We've been at it for 50 years. That's a long time for anything.

And in 2019 Crosby said:

The truth was, CSN, towards the end, wasn't fun, and we didn't like each other. I was not enjoying it at all. I was doing it for a paycheck, and that's just not a good enough reason. If I had stayed there, man, it would have been the end of music for me. It's certainly not an easy thing to do, leaving a really big, successful band. It's kind of like diving off a cliff. But the work I've been doing by myself since splitting with the guys has been like diving off that cliff, and then halfway down suddenly sprouting eagle's wings. That's what it's felt like. I think they should get over it. That's their life, not mine. I just can't wait around. I have to make the best music I can. Right now. Today.

There was a time we thought we were invincible
That we'd go on and on and on and all along
We'd thought we'd do another show and write another song
But I guess we've lost another one, let it slip away…
(Graham Nash, 'Lost Another One')

The Core Collection

Three hundred essential Crosby, Stills and Nash songs.

Recorded in 1962
Stephen Stills: 'Travellin'', released on *Carry On* (box set) (2013)
Recorded in 1963
Les Baxter's Balladeers: 'Baiion', released on single b-side (1963)
The Hollies: '(Ain't That) Just Like Me', released on single a-side (1963)
The Hollies: 'Hey What's Wrong with Me?', released on single b-side (1963)
The Hollies: 'Searchin'', released on single a-side (1963)
The Hollies: 'Whole World Over', released on single b-side (1963)
The Hollies: 'Stay', released on single a-side (1963)
The Hollies: 'Now's the Time', released on single b-side (1963)
Recorded in 1964
The Au Go-Go Singers: 'High Flying Bird', released on *They Call Us the Au Go-Go Singers* (1964)
The Au Go-Go Singers: 'Miss Nellie', released on *They Call Us the Au Go-Go Singers* (1964)
The Hollies: 'You Better Move On', released on *Stay with The Hollies* (1964)
The Hollies: 'Just One Look', released on single a-side (1964)
The Hollies: 'Keep Off That Friend of Mine', released on single b-side (1964)
The Hollies: 'Here I Go Again', released on single a-side (1964)
The Hollies: 'Baby That's All', released on single b-side (1964)
David Crosby: 'Get Together', released on *The Preflyte Sessions* (2011)
David Crosby: 'Brotherhood of the Blues', released on *Byrd Parts, volume 2* (2003)
David Crosby: 'Come Back Baby', released on *The Preflyte Sessions* (2011)
David Crosby: 'Willie Jean', released on *The Preflyte Sessions* (2011)
David Crosby: 'Jack of Diamonds', released on *The Preflyte Sessions* (2011)
The Jet Set: 'The Airport Song', released on *The Preflyte Sessions* (2011)
The Jet Set: 'You Movin'', released on *The Preflyte Sessions* (2011)
The Hollies: 'We're Through', released on single a-side (1964)
The Hollies: 'Come on Back', released on single b-side (1964)
Recorded in 1965
The Hollies: 'Yes I Will', released on single a-side (1965)
The Hollies: 'Nobody', released on single b-side (1965)
The Byrds: 'Mr Tambourine Man', released on single a-side (1965)
The Byrds: 'I Knew I'd Want You', released on single b-side (1965)
The Hollies: 'I'm Alive', released on single a-side (1965)
The Hollies: 'You Know He Did', released on single b-side (1965)
The Byrds: 'Chimes of Freedom', released on single a-side (1965)
The Byrds: 'The Bells of Rhymney', released on single b-side (1965)
The Byrds: 'All I Really Want to Do', released on single a-side (1965)
The Byrds: 'I'll Feel a Whole Lot Better', released on single b-side (1965)
The Hollies: 'Look Through Any Window', released on single a-side (1965)
The Hollies: 'So Lonely', released on single b-side (1965)
The Byrds: 'Turn! Turn! Turn!', released on single a-side (1965)
The Byrds: 'She Don't Care About Time', released on single b-side (1965)
The Hollies: 'If I Needed Someone 'single a-side (1965)
The Hollies: 'I've Got A Way of My Own', released on single b-side (1965)

Recorded in 1966
The Byrds: 'Set You Free This Time', released on single a-side (1966)
The Byrds: 'It Won't Be Wrong', released on single b-side (1966)
The Hollies: 'I Can't Let Go', released on single a-side (1966)
The Hollies: 'Running Through the Night', released on single b-side (1966)
The Byrds: 'Eight Miles High', released on single a-side (1966)
The Byrds: 'Why?', released on single b-side (1966)
The Byrds: '5D (Fifth Dimension)', released on single a-side (1966)
The Byrds: 'Captain Soul', released on single b-side (1966)
The Hollies: 'Bus Stop', released on single a-side (1966)
The Hollies: 'Don't Run and Hide', released on single b-side (1966)
The Hollies: 'I Am A Rock', released on *Would You Believe?* (1966)
The Byrds: 'Psychodrama City', released on *Never Before*(1990)
The Byrds: 'Mr Spaceman', released on single a-side (1966)
The Byrds: 'What's Happening?!?!', released on single b-side (1966)
The Hollies: 'Stop Stop Stop', released on single a-side (1966)
The Hollies: 'It's You', released on single b-side (1966)
Buffalo Springfield: 'Go and Say Goodbye', released on *Buffalo Springfield* (1966)
Buffalo Springfield: 'Pay the Price', released on *Buffalo Springfield* (1966)
Buffalo Springfield: 'Sit Down I Think I Love You', released on *Buffalo Springfield* (1966)
The Byrds: 'It Happens Each Day', released on *Never Before* (1990)
Buffalo Springfield: 'For What It's Worth', released on single a-side (1967)

Recorded in 1967
The Byrds: 'So You Want Tt Be A Rock and Roll Star', released on single a-side (1967)
The Byrds: 'Everybody's Been Burned', released on single b-side (1967)
The Hollies: 'On A Carousel', released on single a-side (1967)
The Hollies: 'All the World Is Love', released on single b-side (1967)
The Byrds: 'My Back Pages', released on single a-side (1967)
The Byrds: 'Renaissance Fair', released on single b-side (1967)
The Byrds: 'Have You Seen Her Face?', released on single a-side (1967)
The Byrds: 'Don't Make Waves', released on single b-side (1967)
The Hollies: 'Carrie Anne', released on single a-side (1967)
The Hollies: 'Signs That Will Never Change', released on single b-side (1967)
The Hollies: 'Stop Right There', released on *Evolution*(1967)
The Byrds: 'Lady Friend', released on single a-side (1967)
The Byrds: 'Old John Robertson', released on single b-side (1967)
The Hollies: 'King Midas In Reverse', released on single a-side (1967)
The Hollies: 'Everything Is Sunshine', released on single b-side (1967)
Buffalo Springfield: 'Bluebird (full length)', released on *Buffalo Springfield* 2LP compilation (1973)
Buffalo Springfield: 'Everydays', released on *Buffalo Springfield Again* (1967)
Buffalo Springfield: 'Hung Upside Down', released on *Buffalo Springfield Again* (1967)
Buffalo Springfield: 'Pretty Girl Why', released on *Buffalo Springfield Again* (1967)
Buffalo Springfield: 'Rock and Roll Woman', released on *Buffalo Springfield Again* (1967)
The Hollies: 'Away Away Away', released on *Butterfly* (1967)
The Hollies: 'Butterfly', released on *Butterfly* (1967)
The Hollies: 'Dear Eloise', released on *Butterfly* (1967)
The Hollies: 'Maker', released on *Butterfly* (1967)
The Hollies: 'Postcard', released on *Butterfly* (1967)

The Hollies: 'Wishyouawish', released on *Butterfly* (1967)
Recorded in 1968
The Hollies: 'Jennifer Eccles', released on single a-side (1968)
The Hollies: 'Open Up Your Eyes', released on single b-side (1968)
David Crosby: 'Games', released on *Voyage* (box set) (2006)
Stephen Stills: 'Who Ran Away', released on *Carry On* (box set) (2013)
Stephen Stills: 'Judy', released on *Just Roll Tape* (2007)
The Hollies: 'The Times They Are A-Changin'', released on *Clark, Hicks & Nash Years* (box set) (2011)
Buffalo Springfield: 'Four Days Gone', released on *Last Time Around* (1968)
Buffalo Springfield: 'Questions', released on *Last Time Around* (1968)
Buffalo Springfield: 'Special Care', released on *Last Time Around* (1968)
Kooper-Stills: 'It Takes A Lot to Laugh', released on *Supersession* (1968)
The Hollies: 'Man with No Expression', released on *Clark, Hicks & Nash Years* (box set) (2011)
The Hollies: 'Listen to Me', released on single a-side (1968)
The Hollies: 'Do the Best You Can', released on single b-side (1968)
Stephen Stills: '49 Reasons', released on *Carry On* (box set) (2013)
David Crosby: 'Long Time Gone', released on *Voyage* (box set) (2006)
David Crosby: 'Guinnevere', released on *CSN* (box set) (1991)
Recorded in 1969
Crosby, Stills & Nash: 'Suite: Judy Blue Eyes', released on *Crosby, Stills & Nash* (1969)
Crosby, Stills & Nash: 'Helplessly Hoping', released on *Crosby, Stills & Nash* (1969)
Crosby, Stills & Nash: 'Lady of the Island', released on *Crosby, Stills & Nash* (1969)
Crosby, Stills & Nash: 'Marrakesh Express', released on *Crosby, Stills & Nash* (1969)
Crosby, Stills & Nash: 'Pre-Road Downs', released on *Crosby, Stills & Nash* (1969)
Crosby, Stills & Nash: 'Wooden Ships', released on *Crosby, Stills & Nash* (1969)
Crosby, Stills & Nash: 'You Don't Have to Cry', released on *Crosby, Stills & Nash* (1969)
Crosby, Stills & Nash: 'Blackbird', released on *CSN*(box set) (1991)
Crosby, Stills, Nash & Young: '4 + 20', released on *Déjà Vu* (1970)
Crosby, Stills, Nash & Young: 'The Lee Shore', released on *CSN* (box set) (1991)
Stephen Stills featuring Jimi Hendrix: '$20 Fine', released on *Both Sides of the Sky* (2018)
Crosby, Stills, Nash & Young: 'Sea of Madness', released on *The Archives Volume 1: 1963-1972* (2009)
David Crosby & Graham Nash: 'Déjà Vu', released on *Voyage* (box set) (2006)
Crosby, Stills & Nash: 'How Have You Been?', released on *White Knuckle Scorin', released on* (1991)
David Crosby: 'Triad', released on *Voyage* (box set) (2006)
Recorded in 1970
Crosby, Stills, Nash & Young: 'Almost Cut My Hair', released on *Déjà Vu* (1970)
Crosby, Stills, Nash & Young: 'Country Girl', released on *Déjà Vu* (1970)
Crosby, Stills, Nash & Young: 'Helpless', released on *Déjà Vu* (1970)
Crosby, Stills, Nash & Young: 'Our House', released on *Déjà Vu* (1970)
Crosby, Stills, Nash & Young: 'Teach Your Children', released on *Déjà Vu* (1970)
Crosby, Stills, Nash & Young: 'Woodstock', released on *Déjà Vu* (1970)
Crosby, Stills & Nash: 'Carry On [remix]', released on *Replay* (1980)
Crosby, Stills & Nash: 'As I Come of Age', released on *Stills* (1975)
Crosby, Stills, Nash & Young: 'Ohio', released on single a-side (1970)
Crosby, Stills, Nash & Young: 'Find the Cost of Freedom', released on single b-side (1970)

Crosby, Stills, Nash & Young: 'Only Love Can Break Your Heart', released on *The Archives Volume 1: 1963-1972* (2009)
Crosby, Stills, Nash & Young: 'Tell Me Why', released on *The Archives Volume 1: 1963-1972* (2009)
Stephen Stills: 'Black Queen', released on *4 Way Street* (CD reissue) (1992)
Stephen Stills: 'Singin' Call', released on *Stills Alone* (1991)
Stephen Stills: 'Sit Yourself Down', released on *Stephen Stills* (1970)
Stephen Stills: 'Do for the Others', released on *Stephen Stills* (1970)
Stephen Stills: 'Love the One You're With', released on *Stephen Stills* (1970)
Stephen Stills: 'We Are Not Helpless', released on *Stephen Stills* (1970)
David Crosby, Graham Nash & Neil Young: 'Music Is Love', released on *If I Could Only Remember My Name* (1971)

Recorded in 1971

Graham Nash: 'Be Yourself', released on *Songs for Beginners* (1971)
David Crosby: 'Laughing', released on *If I Could Only Remember My Name* (1971)
David Crosby: 'Orleans', released on *If I Could Only Remember My Name* (1971)
David Crosby: 'Traction in the Rain', released on *If I Could Only Remember My Name* (1971)
Graham Nash: 'I Used to Be a King', released on *Songs for Beginners* (1971)
Graham Nash: 'Military Madness', released on *Songs for Beginners* (1971)
Graham Nash: 'Simple Man', released on *Songs for Beginners* (1971)
Graham Nash: 'Sleep Song', released on *Songs for Beginners* (1971)
Stephen Stills: 'Marianne', released on *Stephen Stills 2* (1971)
Stephen Stills: 'Word Game', released on *Stephen Stills 2* (1971)
Stephen Stills: 'Change Partners', released on *Stephen Stills 2* (1971)
David Crosby & Graham Nash: 'Urge for Going', released on *CSN* (box set) (1991)
David Crosby & Graham Nash: 'Man in the Mirror', released on *Another Stoney Evening* (1998)
Graham Nash: 'Stranger's Room', released on *Another Stoney Evening* (1998)

Recorded in 1972

David Crosby & Graham Nash: 'Immigration Man', released on *Graham Nash David Crosby* (1972)
David Crosby & Graham Nash: 'Where Will I Be?', released on *Graham Nash David Crosby* (1972)
David Crosby & Graham Nash: 'Page 43', released on *Graham Nash David Crosby* (1972)
David Crosby & Graham Nash: 'Southbound Train', released on *Graham Nash David Crosby* (1972)
David Crosby & Graham Nash: 'The Wall Song', released on *Graham Nash David Crosby* (1972)
Manassas: 'Song of Love', released on *Manassas* (1972)
Manassas: 'Jet Set (Sigh)', released on *Manassas* (1972)
Manassas: 'Bound to Fall', released on *Manassas* (1972)
Manassas: 'Colorado', released on *Manassas* (1972)
Manassas: 'Johnny's Garden', released on *Manassas* (1972)
Manassas: 'Right Now', released on *Manassas* (1972)
Manassas: 'So Begins the Task', released on *Manassas* (1972)
Manassas: 'Blues Man', released on *Manassas* (1972)

Recorded in 1973

The Byrds: 'Long Live the King', released on *Byrds* (1973)

Crosby, Stills, Nash & Young: 'See the Changes', released on *CSN* (box set) (1991)
Crosby, Stills, Nash & Young: 'Through My Sails', released on *Zuma* (1975)
Manassas: 'Guanganco de Vero', released on *Down the Road* (1973)
Manassas: 'Pensamiento', released on *Down the Road* (1973)
Graham Nash: 'Another Sleep Song', released on *Wild Tales* (1974)
Graham Nash: 'And So It Goes', released on *Wild Tales* (1974)
Graham Nash: 'Grave Concern', released on *Wild Tales* (1974)
Graham Nash: 'Prison Song', released on *Wild Tales* (1974)
Recorded in 1974
Stephen Stills: 'Crossroads-You Can't Catch Me', released on *Live* (1975)
Crosby, Stills, Nash & Young: 'Pushed It Over the End', released on Italian 12' single (1981)
Crosby, Stills, Nash & Young: 'Love Art Blues', released on *CSNY 1974* (2014)
Crosby, Stills, Nash & Young: 'Mellow My Mind', released on *CSNY 1974* (2014)
Crosby, Stills, Nash & Young: 'Traces', released on *CSNY 1974* (2014)
Crosby, Stills, Nash & Young: 'Homeward Thru the Haze', released on *CSN* (box set) (1991)

Recorded in 1975

Stephen Stills: 'Turn Back the Pages', released on *Stills* (1975)
Stephen Stills: 'Cold Cold World', released on *Stills* (1975)
Stephen Stills: 'Myth of Sisyphus', released on *Stills* (1975)
David Crosby & Graham Nash: 'Bittersweet', released on *Wind on the Water* (1975)
David Crosby & Graham Nash: 'Carry Me', released on *Wind on the Water* (1975)
David Crosby & Graham Nash: 'Fieldworker', released on *Wind on the Water* (1975)
David Crosby & Graham Nash: 'Naked in the Rain', released on *Wind on the Water* (1975)
David Crosby & Graham Nash: 'To the Last Whale…', released on *Wind on the Water* (1975)

Recorded in 1976

Stephen Stills: 'Stateline Blues', released on *Illegal Stills* (1976)
Crosby, Stills, Nash & Young: 'Taken at All', released on *CSN* (box set) (1991)
Crosby, Stills, Nash & Young: 'Black Coral', released on *Carry On* (box set) (2013)
Crosby, Stills, Nash & Young: 'Long May You Run', released on *Decade* (1978)
David Crosby & Graham Nash: 'Marguerita', released on *Whistling Down the Wire* (1976)
David Crosby & Graham Nash: 'Out of the Darkness', released on *Whistling Down the Wire* (1976)
David Crosby & Graham Nash: 'Time After Time', released on *Whistling Down the Wire* (1976)
Stills-Young Band: 'Make Love to You', released on *Long May You Run* (1976)
David Crosby & Graham Nash: 'King of the Mountain', released on *Crosby-Nash Live* (CD reissue) (2000)
Crosby, Stills & Nash: 'Just a Song Before I Go', released on *CSN* (1977)

Recorded in 1977

Crosby, Stills & Nash: 'Anything at All', released on *CSN* (1977)
Crosby, Stills & Nash: 'Cold Rain', released on *CSN* (1977)
Crosby, Stills & Nash: 'Fair Game', released on *CSN* (1977)
Crosby, Stills & Nash: 'In My Dreams', released on *CSN* (1977)
Crosby, Stills & Nash: 'I Give You Give Blind' (remix) released on *Replay* (1980)

Crosby, Stills & Nash: 'He Played Real Good for Free', released on *Allies* (1983)
Crosby, Stills & Nash: 'Shadow Captain', released on *Allies* (1983)

Recorded in 1978

Stephen Stills: 'Beaucoup Yumbo', released on *Thoroughfare Gap* (1978)
Stephen Stills: 'Thorofare Gap', released on *Thoroughfare Gap* (1978)

Recorded in 1979

Stephen Stills: 'Spanish Suite', released on *Man Alive!* (2008)

Recorded in 1980

David Crosby: 'Samurai', released on *Voyage* (box set) (2006)
David Crosby: 'Might as Well Have a Good Time', released on *Daylight Again* (CD reissue) (2006)
Crosby, Stills & Nash: 'Delta', released on *Daylight Again* (1982)
Crosby, Stills & Nash: 'Southern Cross', released on *Daylight Again* (1982)
Crosby, Stills & Nash: 'Turn Your Back on Love', released on *Daylight Again* (1982)
Crosby, Stills & Nash: 'Wasted on the Way', released on *Daylight Again* (1982)

Recorded in 1983

The Hollies: 'Take My Love and Run', released on *What Goes Around ...* (1983)
Crosby, Stills & Nash: 'Raise a Voice', released on *Allies* (1983)
Crosby, Stills & Nash: 'War Games', released on *Allies* (1983)

Recorded in 1984

Stephen Stills: 'No Hiding Place', released on *Right by You* (1984)

Recorded in 1985

Graham Nash 'Glass and Steel', released on *Innocent Eyes* (1985)

Recorded in 1987

Crosby, Stills & Nash: 'Chuck's Lament', released on *Amazing Grace & Chuck* (soundtrack) (1990)

Recorded in 1988

Crosby, Stills, Nash & Young: 'American Dream', released on *American Dream* (1988)
Crosby, Stills, Nash & Young: 'Compass', released on *American Dream* (1988)
Crosby, Stills, Nash & Young: 'Feel Your Love', released on *American Dream* (1988)
David Crosby: 'Tracks in the Dust', released on *Oh Yes I Can* (1989)

Recorded in 1989

David Crosby: 'In the Wide Ruin', released on *Oh Yes I Can* (1989)
David Crosby: 'My Country 'Tis of Thee', released on *Oh Yes I Can* (1989)
David Crosby: 'Oh Yes I Can', released on *Oh Yes I Can* (1989)
CSN + James Taylor: 'Chippin', released on Away', released on CD single (1989)

Recorded in 1990

The Byrds: 'He Was A Friend of Mine', released on *The Byrds* (box set) (1990)
Crosby, Stills & Nash: 'After the Dolphin', released on *Live It Up* (1990)
Crosby, Stills & Nash: 'Arrows', released on *Live It Up* (1990)
Crosby, Stills & Nash: 'Haven't We Lost Enough?', released on *Live It Up* (1990)
Crosby, Stills & Nash: 'House of Broken Dreams', released on *Live It Up* (1990)
Crosby, Stills & Nash: 'Yours and Mine', released on *Live It Up* (1990)

Recorded in 1991

Stephen Stills: 'Ballad of Hollis Brown', released on *Stills Alone* (1991)
Stephen Stills: 'Treetop Flyer', released on *Stills Alone* (1991)

Recorded in 1993

David Crosby: 'Thousand Roads', released on *Thousand Roads* (1993)
David Crosby: 'Yvette In English', released on *Thousand Roads* (1993)

David Crosby: 'Hero', released on *Thousand Roads* (1993)
David Crosby: 'Til It Shines on You', released on *It's All Coming Back to Me Now* (1995)
Recorded in 1994
Crosby, Stills & Nash: 'After the Storm', released on *After the Storm* (1994)
Crosby, Stills & Nash: 'Camera', released on *After the Storm* (1994)
Crosby, Stills & Nash: 'Find a Dream', released on *After the Storm* (1994)
Recorded in 1997
CPR: 'Somehow She Knew', released on *Live at Cuesta College* (1998)
Recorded in 1998
Crosby, Stills & Nash: 'Half Your Angels', released on promo download (2001)
Crosby, Stills, Nash & Young: 'Heartland', released on *Looking Forward* (1999)
Crosby, Stills, Nash & Young: 'Faith in Me', released on *Looking Forward* (1999)
CPR: 'Morrison', released on *CPR* (1999)
CPR: 'Time is the Final Currency', released on *CPR* (1999)
CPR: 'Rusty and Blue', released on *Live at the Wiltern* (1999)
Recorded in 1999
Crosby, Stills, Nash & Young: 'Looking Forward', released on *Looking Forward* (1999)
Crosby, Stills, Nash & Young: 'Stand and Be Counted', released on *Looking Forward* (1999)
Crosby, Stills, Nash & Young: 'Climber', released on *Voyage* (box set) (2006)
Crosby, Stills, Nash & Young: 'Seen Enough', released on *Looking Forward* (1999)
Crosby, Stills, Nash & Young: 'Someday Soon', released on *Looking Forward* (1999)
Recorded in 2000
CPR: 'Map to Buried Treasure', released on *Just Like Gravity* (2000)
CPR: 'Just Like Gravity', released on *Just Like Gravity* (2000)
Graham Nash: 'Try to Find Me', released on *Reflections* (box set) (2009)
Graham Nash: 'Dirty Little Secret', released on Songs for *Survivors* (2002)
Graham Nash: 'Chelsea Hotel', released on Songs for *Survivors* (2002)
Graham Nash: 'Pavanne', released on Songs for *Survivors* (2002)
Recorded in 2002
Crosby, Stills, Nash & Young: 'Dream for Him', released on *Voyage* (box set) (2006)
Recorded in 2004
David Crosby & Graham Nash: 'Jesus of Rio', released on *Crosby*Nash* (2004)
David Crosby & Graham Nash: 'Don't Dig Here', released on *Crosby*Nash* (2004)
David Crosby & Graham Nash: 'Lay Me Down', released on *Crosby*Nash* (2004)
David Crosby & Graham Nash: 'Puppeteer', released on *Crosby*Nash* (2004)
David Crosby & Graham Nash: 'Through Here Quite Often', released on *Crosby*Nash* (2004)
Stephen Stills: 'Ain't It Always', released on *Carry On* (box set) (2013)
Recorded in 2005
Stephen Stills: 'Different Man', released on *Man Alive!* (2005)
Stephen Stills: 'Piece of Me', released on *Man Alive!* (2005)
Stephen Stills: 'Round the Bend', released on *Man Alive!* (2005)
Recorded in 2006
Crosby, Stills, Nash & Young: 'Let's Impeach the President', released on *Déjà Vu Live* (2008)
Crosby, Stills, Nash & Young: 'Living with War', released on *Déjà Vu Live* (2008)
Recorded in 2007
Graham Nash: 'In Your Name', released on *Reflections* (box set) (2009)

Recorded in 2008
Stephen Stills: 'Blind Fiddler', released on *Live at Shepherd's Bush* (2009)
Stephen Stills: 'Isn't It About Time', released on *Live at Shepherd's Bush* (2009)
Recorded in 2011
Graham Nash: 'Raining in My Heart', released on *Rave On* (2011)
Graham Nash & James Raymond: 'Almost Gone (The Ballad of Bradley Manning)', released on download (2011)
Recorded in 2012
Crosby, Stills & Nash: 'Girl from the North Country', released on *CSN 2012* (2012)
Crosby, Stills & Nash: 'Radio', released on *CSN 2012* (2012)
Recorded in 2013
The Rides: 'Can't Get Enough of Your Love', released on *Can't Get Enough* (2013)
The Rides: 'Don't Want Lies', released on *Can't Get Enough* (2013)
The Rides: 'Only Teardrops Fall', released on *Can't Get Enough* (2013)
The Rides: 'Roadhouse', released on *Can't Get Enough* (2013)
Recorded in 2014
David Crosby: 'Morning Falling', released on *Croz* (2014)
David Crosby: 'The Clearing', released on *Croz* (2014)
David Crosby: 'What's Broken', released on *Croz* (2014)
Recorded in 2016
Graham Nash: 'Golden Days', released on *This Path Tonight* (2016)
Graham Nash: 'Myself at Last', released on *This Path Tonight* (2016)
Graham Nash: 'This Path Tonight', released on *This Path Tonight* (2016)
Graham Nash: 'Mississippi Burning', released on *This Path Tonight* deluxe edition (2016)
The Rides: 'Kick out of It', released on *Pierced Arrow* (2016)
The Rides: 'There Was a Place', released on *Pierced Arrow* (2016)
The Rides: 'Virtual World', released on *Pierced Arrow* (2016)
Snarky Puppy featuring David Crosby: 'Somebody Home' from *Family Dinner – Volume 2* (2016)
David Crosby: 'By the Light of Common Day', released on *Lighthouse* (2016)
David Crosby: 'Things We Do for Love', released on *Lighthouse* (2016)
Recorded in 2017
David Crosby: 'She's Got to Be Somewhere', released on *Sky Trails* (2017)
David Crosby: 'Sky Trails', released on *Sky Trails* (2017)
Recorded in 2018
David Crosby, Michael League, Becca Stevens and Michelle Willis: 'Balanced on a Pin', released on *Here If You Listen* (2018)
David Crosby, Michael League, Becca Stevens and Michelle Willis: 'Glory', released on *Here If You Listen* (2018)

Bibliography

Browne, D., *Fire and Rain: The Beatles, Simon and Garfunkel, James Taylor, CSNY, and the Lost Story of 1970* (Da Capo, New York, 2011)

Crosby, Stills, Nash & Young: The Wild, Definitive Saga of Rock's Greatest Supergroup (Da Capo, New York, 2019)

Christgau, R., *Christgau's Guide: Rock Albums of the Seventies* (Vermilion, London, 1982)

Collins, J. *Sweet Judy Blue Eyes: My Life in Music* (Crown Archetype, New York, 2011)

Crosby, D. and Gottleib, C. *Long Time Gone: The Autobiography of David Crosby* (Doubleday, New York, 1988)

Since Then: How I Survived Everything and Lived to Tell About It (Berkeley Publishing, New York, 2006)

Diltz, H., *California Dreaming* (Genesis Publications, Guildford, 2007)

Doggett, P. *Crosby, Stills, Nash & Young: The Biography* (Simon & Schuster, New York, 2019)

Frame, P. *Rock Family Trees* (Omnibus Press, London, 1980)

Glatt, J., *Live at the Fillmore East and West: Getting Backstage and Personal with Rock's Greatest Legends* (Lyons Press, Guildford CT, 2015)

Kruger, D., unpublished interview with Graham Nash at www.debbiekruger.com, quotes used with permission

Johns, G.,*Sound Man* (Blue Rider Press, New York, 2014)

Logan, N. and Woffinden, B. (eds) *The Illustrated 'New Musical Express' Encyclopaedia of Rock*, revised edition (Salamander Books, London, 1977)

McGowan, D., *Weird Scenes Inside the Canyon: Laurel Canyon, Covert Ops and the Dark Heart of the Hippie Dream* (Headpress, Truro, 2014)

Nash, G.,*Wild Tales: A Rock and Roll Life* (Viking, London, 2013)

Pattinson, A., *The Alan's Album Archives Guide to the Music of...Crosby, Stills, Nash and (Sometimes) Young: 'Change Partners'* (SpareRoom Studios, 2018)

Perone, J., *Smash Hits: The 100 Songs That Defined America* (Greenwood, Santa Barbara, 2016)

Rogan, J. *Crosby, Stills, Nash & Young: The Visual Documentary* (Omnibus, London, 1996)

Neil Young: Zero to Sixty (Rogan House, London, 2000)

Roberts, D., *Stephen Stills: Change Partners* (Red Planet, Falmouth, 2016)

Spitz, B., *Barefoot in Babylon: The Creation of the Woodstock Festival 1969* (Viking, New York, 1979 / 2014)

Taylor, D. *Prisoner of Woodstock* (Thunders Mouth Press, New York, 1994)

Verbaka, H. et al *Crosby, Stills, Nash & Sometimes Young vol 3.* (Gopher, Gronigen, 2002)

Yaffe, D., *Reckless Daughter: A Portrait of Joni Mitchell* (Sarah Crichton Books, New York, 2017)

Young, N. *Waging Heavy Peace: A Hippie Dream* (Viking, London, 2012)

Zimmer, D. *Crosby, Stills and Nash: The Biography* (Da Capo, New York, 1984 / 2008)

Four Way Street: The Crosby, Stills, Nash & Young Reader (Da Capo, New York, 2004)

On Track series

Queen – Andrew Wild 978-1-78952-003-3
Emerson Lake and Palmer – Mike Goode 978-1-78952-000-2
Deep Purple and Rainbow 1968-79 – Steve Pilkington 978-1-78952-002-6
Yes – Stephen Lambe 978-1-78952-001-9
Blue Oyster Cult – Jacob Holm-Lupo 978-1-78952-007-1
The Beatles – Andrew Wild 978-1-78952-009-5
Roy Wood and the Move – James R Turner 978-1-78952-008-8
Genesis – Stuart MacFarlane 978-1-78952-005-7
JethroTull – Jordan Blum 978-1-78952-016-3
The Rolling Stones 1963-80 – Steve Pilkington 978-1-78952-017-0
Judas Priest – John Tucker 978-1-78952-018-7
Toto – Jacob Holm-Lupo 978-1-78952-019-4
Van Der Graaf Generator – Dan Coffey 978-1-78952-031-6
Frank Zappa 1966 to 1979 – Eric Benac 978-1-78952-033-0
Elton John in the 1970s – Peter Kearns 978-1-78952-034-7
The Moody Blues – Geoffrey Feakes 978-1-78952-042-2
The Beatles Solo 1969-1980 – Andrew Wild 978-1-78952-030-9
Steely Dan – Jez Rowden 978-1-78952-043-9
Hawkwind – Duncan Harris 978-1-78952-052-1
Fairport Convention – Kevan Furbank 978-1-78952-051-4
Iron Maiden – Steve Pilkington 978-1-78952-061-3
Dream Theater – Jordan Blum 978-1-78952-050-7
10CC – Peter Kearns 978-1-78952-054-5
Gentle Giant – Gary Steel 978-1-78952-058-3
Kansas – Kevin Cummings 978-1-78952-057-6
Mike Oldfield – Ryan Yard 978-1-78952-060-6
The Who – Geoffrey Feakes 978-1-78952-076-7

On Screen series

Carry On… – Stephen Lambe 978-1-78952-004-0
Powell and Pressburger – Sam Proctor 978-1-78952-013-2
Seinfeld Seasons 1 to 5 – Stephen Lambe 978-1-78952-012-5
Francis Ford Coppola – Cam Cobb and Stephen Lambe 978-1-78952-022-4
Monty Python – Steve Pilkington 978-1-78952-047-7
Doctor Who: The David Tennant Years – Jamie Hailstone 978-1-78952-066-8
James Bond – Andrew Wild 978-1-78952-010-1

Other Books

Not As Good As The Book – Andy Tillison 978-1-78952-021-7
The Voice. Frank Sinatra in the 1940s – Stephen Lambe 978-1-78952-032-3
Maximum Darkness – Deke Leonard 978-1-78952-048-4
The Twang Dynasty – Deke Leonard 978-1-78952-049-1
Maybe I Should've Stayed In Bed – Deke Leonard 978-1-78952-053-8
Tommy Bolin: In and Out of Deep Purple – Laura Shenton 978-1-78952-070-5
Jon Anderson and the Warriors - the road to Yes – David Watkinson 978-1-78952-059-0

and many more to come!

Would you like to write for Sonicbond Publishing?

We are mainly a music publisher, but we also occasionally publish in other genres including film and television. At Sonicbond Publishing we are always on the look-out for authors, particularly for our two main series, On Track and Decades.

Mixing fact with in depth analysis, the On Track series examines the entire recorded work of a particular musical artist or group. All genres are considered from easy listening and jazz to 60s soul to 90s pop, via rock and metal.

The Decades series singles out a particular decade in an artist or group's history and focuses on that decade in more detail than may be allowed in the On Track series.

While professional writing experience would, of course, be an advantage, the most important qualification is to have real enthusiasm and knowledge of your subject. First-time authors are welcomed, but the ability to write well in English is essential.

Sonicbond Publishing has distribution throughout Europe and North America, and all our books are also published in E-book form. Authors will be paid a royalty based on sales of their book. Further details about our books are available from www.sonicbondpublishing.com. To contact us, complete the contact form there or email info@sonicbondpublishing.co.uk